Visions in the Night

Visions in the Night

Hearing God in your dreams

RUSS PARKER

Originally published in Great Britain in 2002
as *Dream Stories: A journey into the Bible's dreams and visions*
by the Bible Reading Fellowship

This edition published in Great Britain in 2013

Society for Promoting Christian Knowledge
36 Causton Street
London SW1P 4ST
www.spckpublishing.co.uk

British Library Cataloguing-in-Publication Data
A catalogue record for this book is available from the British Library

ISBN 978–0–281–07083–1
eBook ISBN 978–0–281–07084–8

Typeset by Graphicraft Limited, Hong Kong
First printed in Great Britain by Ashford Colour Press
Subsequently digitally printed in Great Britain

eBook by Graphicraft Limited, Hong Kong

Produced on paper from sustainable forests

With many thanks to
Fiona Gibbon, Esther Langrish,
Julia Johnson and Maggie Curtis
who have been a marvellous dream team

Contents

Contents

Introduction

Not so long ago I took part in a healing and reconciliation event with three Roman Catholic churches in the town of Drogheda in the Republic of Ireland. I had been invited, at very short notice, to give a brief address at each morning service of the Mass. As I prayed about what to say in my brief five minutes, it was impressed upon me that I should lead an apology on behalf of the English for the hundreds of years of domination our nation had exercised in that country. Initially, I fought against this conviction, partly because I am of no real importance or standing in my own country, and partly because the event in question was surely a thing of the past and what good would my apology do?

I couldn't have been more wrong! Following each apology there was a tremendous outpouring of tears and applause. Both clergy and congregational members told me that this was so long overdue and they were grateful I had done it. So much so that this sparked off a real determination to build better relationships with the Protestant churches in the town and a commitment to healing and ecumenism.

It was shortly after this that I had a telephone call from a stranger who said that he had had a recurring dream that he was to go to the town of Drogheda and lead an apology on behalf of his ancestors and the damage they had contributed to that town. The man in question was a descendant of Oliver Cromwell whose troops had burnt to death many people in one of the Catholic churches of that time.

I shared my recent experience in Ireland and in due course this man went there to lead an apology on behalf of his family. All this helped to make possible a healing of the historical wounds and a transformation of attitudes towards non-Catholics in Drogheda.

This was another confirmation for me of the importance of dreams, not just for our personal growth but also for those times when God uses our ability to dream to inspire and challenge us to hear his word of direction in our lives. The Bible is full of examples of people to whom God spoke in this way. Consider the prophetic dreams warning of forthcoming famine that Pharaoh had, the challenges to the despot ruler Nebuchadnezzar to acknowledge properly that the real power behind his throne was the favour of God, how God inspired a host of prophets to speak out the things they had seen and heard in the visions they received, and how the holy family evaded the murder of Jesus through a dream given to both the Magi and Joseph.

Far from being a fringe topic in the Scriptures, dreams and visions play a central role in the unfolding purposes of God. There are over one hundred and thirty references to dreams and over one hundred to visions. In the wake of the current growth of Charismatic churches has come a renewed passion for experiencing the prophetic outpouring of God's Spirit and the visions needed to build a new way of being the church that serves its community. It is surely this focus which has made popular the recent explosion of training in dream work so typical of such leading providers in church expansion as Bethel Church in Reading, California. Here John Paul Jones has an academy of the supernatural in which training in how to interpret dreams features as part of the curriculum.

In addition to the visionary and missional aspect of dream work, there is also the personal growth factor. I have found from many years of practice and experience that working with our dreams offers us greater insight into who we really think we are and also into the issues that shape us either in recent encounters or from further back in our individual history. This was brought home very powerfully when I took part in a *Songs of Praise* programme devoted to my work with dreams. The BBC film crew recorded, with permission, the dream work of those attending the conference which was at the heart of the broadcast. They managed to capture on camera a number of people who found significant insight, release and healing from their session. Following this I, and some of the team I worked with, received a host of telephone calls from people around the UK who had challenging dreams they longed to unpack and understand.

Consequently, this book is an exploration into some of the ways in which God uses our dreams as the doorway through which he invites us to know ourselves and also to hear his visionary challenges to our lives. We shall be looking at some of the Bible's dream and vision stories and learning how these transformed the lives and the ministries of those who had them. This will give us some insights into our own dream encounters and teach us how to listen out for the voice of God speaking to us through visions of the night.

1

The power of holy places
Jacob's dream at Bethel

———◆•◆•◆———

'Surely the Lord is in this place!'   *Genesis 28:16 (NRSV)*

The dream

In a dream, he saw a ladder that reached from earth to heaven,
and God's angels were going up and down on it. The Lord
was standing beside the ladder and said: 'I am the Lord God
who was worshipped by Abraham and Isaac. I will give to your
family the land on which you are now sleeping. Your descendants
will spread over the earth in all directions and will become
numerous as the specks of dust. Your family will be a blessing
to all people. Wherever you go, I will watch over you, then
later I will bring you back to this land. I won't leave you—I
will do all I have promised.'   *Genesis 28:12–15 (CEV)*

By any standards, this is a very encouraging dream for Jacob, but
it is more specifically a prophetic dream. Although Jacob is sleeping and dreaming, God steps into the dream process with his own
words of prophetic challenge. We should not be surprised by this,
because we believe in a God who speaks to his people. Consequently
it is to be expected that, as we create our dreams in our sleep, the
Creator God in whose image we are made weaves his words and
visions of revelation within and around our own thoughts. The
Bible contains a wealth of such examples, ranging from Solomon's
dream interview with God at the time of the building of the first
temple (1 Kings 3:5–14) to the rooftop vision of Peter which
changed the whole course of the Church's mission (Acts 10:9–20).

1

In Old Testament days, such dreams and visions were thought to be limited to prophets and seers, but with the coming of the Holy Spirit at the birth of the Church such gifts were now available for the young and for the mature (Acts 2:17: the term 'old men' is not a suitable translation of the word *presbyter* which occurs here and is usually translated as 'elder' or 'spiritual leader').

The focus of Jacob's prophetic dream is one of promise and guidance. He is reminded of the promises made to his father and grandfather, and the dream contains the added encouragement that the day will dawn when he will return home to see those promises fulfilled.

The story behind the dream

Jacob is on the run. He has made a mess of his home life by trying to swindle his older brother out of his birthright and deceiving his blind father into blessing the wrong son. In all of this he has been aided and abetted by his mother, Rebecca. Behind these episodes is the dangerous habit of parental favouritism that split the children apart and baptized them into a bitter feud of rivalry and striving for domination over each other. Isaac much preferred the adventurous Esau, who loved to hunt and bring home his trophies to a proud father. Jacob found his comfort in remaining close to his mother, while she filled his head with dreams of what might be. This was a recipe for disaster.

At his birth, the younger son had been given the name Jacob, which means 'supplanter', or, in modern jargon, 'con-man'. He had certainly lived up to his name and now he is homeless and a refugee, on his way to work for an uncle he has never met. We have no evidence from the Genesis account that Jacob was ashamed or sorry for his actions, and so we can only wonder how he felt to be so suddenly dispossessed of a family and the comforts of home. Though the terrain may have been familiar to him, and he belonged to a nomadic people, everything would have been threatening as he was quite alone and without protection for the journey. And so, he makes for a familiar place, Bethel, where his grandfather Abraham had been before and had set up an altar to worship God (Genesis 12:8). The place, described in the Revised English Bible (REB) as a 'shrine' (Genesis 28:11), is soon to become more than familiar—it is to be discovered as a holy place.

Learning the dream message

Genesis 28:12–17 is the first dream vision in the Bible, and you could not find a more unlikely candidate for this favour from God than Jacob. At the heart of the dream is the all-consuming truth that God is truly Immanu-el, the God who is with us. For the deserter at Bethel, it is a reminder that God has not deserted him. This intimacy of God with the broken is illustrated by the symbol of the ladder or stairway connecting heaven and earth, alive with angels travelling up and down on it. It reveals to us that God is continually connected to his world and constantly wishes to bring his word to it. The ladder symbolism is fulfilled in Jesus, who described his own ministry as the movement of angels ascending and descending upon the Son of Man (John 1:51).

The dream also shows us God standing by Jacob: surely the first step on a journey to recovery and healing is always the recognition that God cares for us. It was this truth that empowered the woman caught in adultery to believe she could be forgiven (John 8:1–11), and helped the apostle Peter to fight off the drastic conclusion that he was no longer worth anything because he had denied Jesus (Mark 16:6–7).

Before God makes Jacob any promises, he reveals himself to be the God worshipped by Isaac and Abraham. It is important to realize what this revelation does for Jacob. It means that whatever his misdemeanours, he still belongs to the family to whom God has made promises. He may have tried to cheat his brother out of the right of the firstborn but there is no way he can force God to bless him. Yet God comes and reminds him that he still belongs within the family and can therefore hope for a healed future.

The promises that God gives to Jacob take the form of a renewed covenant, similar to those made with Isaac and Abraham (Genesis 28:13–14), a commitment to bring Jacob back home and a promise to be with this lonely wanderer for the rest of his life (28:15). The first thing to notice is how the dream message fits into the current circumstances of the dreamer. He has no place or land to call his own, he is single and homeless, and he is alone. God's promises exactly match his needs. Jacob would no doubt have known the promises to his forefathers that their descendants would be as numerous as the specks of sand and that they would occupy the land as far as the eye could see and be a blessing to nations. Now he too is included in this fantastic gift.

I remember listening to a Mother Superior talking with a person who felt that she had made a colossal mess of her life and could not believe that God could love her at all for what she had done. After a few moments to take in this rather deadly conclusion, the Mother Superior said, 'Well, dear, you have to make your mind up about something, then. Which is the greater, your capacity to make a mess of your life or God's capacity to love you?' After an even longer pause to consider, I am happy to say that the person in question chose God's capacity to love, and her life moved forward.

The very fact that God gave Jacob this renewed promise must have brought hope and healing to a man all too aware that he did not deserve it. His heart must have jumped at the prospect of returning home some day (see Genesis 28: 20–22); and surrounding it all was the dizzy reality that God would always be with him. Such a realization was to become the inner strength that helped him to face up to his own inner demons and the many difficult decisions he would need to make on the journey that lay ahead. It is what gave him patience while he served 20 years as a shepherd for his greedy uncle Laban, who tricked him into marrying a woman he did not love (Genesis 29—31). It was the ultimate reality that stripped him of his scheming instincts and brought him to wrestle face to face with God and confront the fears he had always carried about his brother Esau, who, he was convinced, wanted to murder him (Genesis 32).

Following the dream

The greatest impact that the dream had upon Jacob was the realization that he had been in a holy place and had met with God there. He later described it as 'the gate of heaven' (Genesis 28:17, NJB). His first words upon waking were a confession that God was in that place—and that he had not known it when he first arrived. The God who surprises had been loitering with the intent to bless and redeem. The REB says that Jacob was 'awestruck' and the New American Bible (NAB) says that he was filled with 'solemn wonder' (28:17). Obviously the dream was a profound emotional experience which disturbed him greatly, but it led to decisive action. Like his ancestors before him he set up a stone altar and made vows of commitment and service to God (28:18–22). Here he was connecting with the holy place and setting it aside as a place where he would come especially to worship God. (In fact, he returned here in the future to recharge his vision of God and renew his commitment: see Genesis 35.) He even renamed the place 'Bethel', which means 'house of God'. It seems that the location's former name, Luz, could mean 'to be crafty or deceitful'; and if this is so, the change of name seems to signify a desire for a change of heart in Jacob's future life, no matter how difficult this was to prove. The man who formerly tried to take what was not his own now takes hold of God's promise and offers to give God a tenth of whatever he has. At this moment, the offer amounts to a tenth of nothing, yet God gladly accepts it!

It is interesting to note that this was not the last occasion when Jacob heard the word of God. There were at least four others later in his life (Genesis 31:3; 35:1 and 9; 46:2). However, this first dream came like a bolt in the dark, and because he took it to heart and acted upon it, his life was transformed for ever. Ultimately, he was changed from being Jacob the con-man or supplanter to become Israel, the one whom God esteems as straight and honourable (Genesis 32:28).

Making it personal

We all need holy places where we can connect and engage intimately with the living God and rediscover direction from him. Jacob's experience is typical of the lives of many of the saints who have found closeness to God in all manner of places. The history of the Celtic Christians is filled with such examples: Ninian prayed in his remote cave on the coast near Whithorn; Cuthbert felt at home in his single retreat on the island of Inner Farne; and Columba preferred the wild shores of remote Iona. None was running away from the world, all were seeking holy places to meet with God and be envisioned to meet the needs of a wounded world. Jesus, of course, visited the garden of Gethsemane on more than one occasion and it seems to have been the place where he could face up to difficult decisions (Luke 22:39).

What, then, is a holy place? It is a place where, for us, God has touched the earth with something of heaven. It is a place where God speaks his word and gives vision and renewal for our commitment to him. Such places can be very varied—from the former Airport Vineyard church in Toronto to the shrine at Lourdes. Each has its own distinctive message and ministry and there comes a time in all our lives when we need to renew our intimacy with God and our sense of direction from him.

Based on Jacob's experience at Bethel, we can see that a holy place is where we are fuelled by worship and wonder. I am quite sure that the dearth of visions among God's people is due to a lack of worship and wonder at the majesty and awesomeness of God. Holy places help us to sharpen the focus of our faith on the living God who wishes to draw us into the intimacy of his heart, from which we discover visions of his purposes. Jacob responded by making a vow to follow God, because he was convinced of God's power and care for him. Doubtless we all get worn down by the cares of this world, the messes we sometimes make in our lives and the doubts and disbelief that sap our faith. Consequently, we need to find places where it is easier to connect with God again and be refreshed.

We do not have to travel far to find our holy place. Of course there might be a time when we need to make pilgrimage to a particular holy place because the message and ministry attached to that place are just what we need. We can make space in our own home, however, or in some nearby place in the countryside which is special for us. Like Jacob, we can set aside this place by erecting something that helps us to focus our attention on the presence of God. We can consecrate it by anointing it with oil or clean water as a symbol of the life-giving Spirit to whom we are open each time we come to meet with God. We come to these places to listen and be aware that God is still with us and lives among the broken and the guilty.

In our troubled cities and towns, it is becoming more and more important to have holy places which remind the inhabitants that God is still near. I was particularly blessed recently when I learnt that Bishop Michael Marshall, the (former) Rector of Holy Trinity, Sloane Street in London, had decided to open the church every day so that people could come in to pray and be still and know the presence of God. The building had usually been closed through the day before his arrival, but he was determined that this church was going to become a healing resource to the community and a declaration of God's presence in the city. It reminded me of one of the stories to emerge surrounding the tragic death of Diana, Princess of Wales. One evening, there was a knock on the door of one of the clergymen responsible for the upkeep of a certain cathedral. When he opened the door to see who was there, he was confronted by a woman who was keen to get into the church for reasons she could not really explain. She was so upset by the death of Diana that she just wanted to be in church, near to God, to find some peace of mind. The clergyman repeatedly told the woman that the cathedral was now locked and that she was welcome to come back in the morning. Then the woman said that he had better tell that to the others. When the man stepped outside to see who these 'others' were, he found a large crowd of people who also wanted to get inside the cathedral so that they too could better handle their painful feelings. The clergyman quickly realized that he was missing something important; the wounded often need a holy place where they can offload their struggles and find a way forward.

Prayer

O Lord, when I am rushed and racing through,
find for me
a place where I can be still,
a time to stay in touch with heaven's will,
a corner to cradle my troubled wail,
a mountain to see each city's shadowed vale,
a garden for dialogue and painful decisions,
a space where your word gives visions,
a quiet place, a screaming place,
a healing place and a holy place.
Amen

2

Getting personal with the prophetic

Joseph's home dreams

Joseph had a dream and promptly reported the details to his brothers, causing them to hate him even more.

Genesis 37:5 (NLT)

The dream

Once Joseph had a dream, and when he told it to his brothers, they hated him even more. He said to them, 'Listen to this dream that I dreamed. There we were, binding sheaves in the field. Suddenly my sheaf rose and stood upright; then your sheaves gathered around it, and bowed down to my sheaf.' His brothers said to him, 'Are you indeed to reign over us?' . . . He had another dream . . . 'Look . . . the sun, the moon, and eleven stars were bowing down to me.' . . . His father rebuked him, and said to him, 'What kind of dream is this that you have had? Shall we indeed come, I and your mother and your brothers, and bow to the ground before you?'

Genesis 37:5–10 (NRSV)

At first glance, these two dreams of Joseph's seem to be a mixture of family squabbling and a misplaced sense of importance. Never once are we told that they are dreams from God, nor does Joseph claim that he is God's messenger. However, F. Delitzsch, in his commentary on Genesis, says that we must not be misled into thinking that these are simply the pure flights of fantasy from an ambitious heart, but rather the presentiments of deep inward feelings.[1] It is a fact of life that God often speaks his word through signs, wonders and dreams into the most imperfect of lives. We would rather he chose clearly identifiable people whose lives stand out for God and whose spiritual authenticity is beyond question. Yet where would we be without the likes of Solomon, who complicated his life with many concubines and dabbled in other religions; or Samson, who compromised his calling to be set apart for God and lost his once-incredible strength? There is also Peter, who shared the confidences of Jesus but nevertheless blasphemed when put to the test. None of these characters was perfect, and all were complicated people, but God chose to give them insights into his wonderful purposes and powers.

Joseph's home dreams are a combination of his own story and the prophetic insights which can always come alongside us and our circumstances. It is apparent that he confused the stirrings of God with his exaggerated sense of self-importance within the family. In other words, he put himself at the centre of the prophetic insights that God was giving him, making them too personal and losing sight of the very important need to honour God, not himself.

The story behind the dream

If you were a social worker or a family therapist visiting Joseph's home, you would not take long to conclude that it was only a matter of time before somebody got hurt. There seem to be three basic ingredients to this family's breakdown—parental favouritism, sibling rivalry and a child leaving home.

Parental favouritism

We are told that Jacob loved Joseph more than all his other sons (Genesis 37:3) because he was the first child of Rachel, Jacob's real love. You may recall that when Jacob went to work for his scheming uncle Laban, he immediately fell in love with Rachel, but was fooled into first marrying her older and less attractive sister Leah (Genesis 29:15–25). It is perfectly understandable that the pent-up feelings of desire for a child with Rachel were poured out on Joseph, when he finally arrived in Jacob's old age, in an over-indulgent manner. Unfortunately, Jacob was sowing seeds of division within the family. We should not be surprised that this happened, because Jacob himself was the object of his mother's affections while his father Isaac preferred his older brother, Esau. Parental favouritism had been sown in him from his earliest days and it seems that he was passing this destructive seed to the next generation in his son Joseph.

Sibling rivalry

The indulgent love of his father produced a child who was inflated with his own importance. Joseph was given the fabled coat of many colours as a sign of favour (37:3). The New Jerusalem Bible (NJB) describes it as a 'decorated tunic' and the REB calls it a 'coat with long sleeves'. Delitzsch says that it was probably an outer coat reaching to the wrists and ankles, such as noblemen and kings' daughters wore.[2] By whatever standards, this was certainly an extravagant gift and may even have signalled the right of succession, which would certainly have aroused the antagonism of Joseph's elder brothers. Yet the problem of excessive love and favour was compounded by Joseph's sense of superiority to his brothers. His story opens with the comment that he was seventeen years old, which may suggest all the impulsiveness of youth. He spied on his brothers and brought bad reports of them to his father (37:2). This was hardly a recipe for brotherly bonding! So when he shared his dreams with them, they hated him all the more.

A child leaves home

The hatred of the elder brothers spills over into a plot to kill Joseph, hastily revised to selling him into slavery. There is an added irony in this, of course: Joseph had been boasting of his special place in his father's affections, and now he would be a slave, the lowest of the low. How many other family breakdowns could we attribute to the unwise and obsessional smothering love of a mother or father?

Learning the dream message

There are two separate dreams to explore here. Undoubtedly the first dream paints a picture of the supremacy of Joseph over his brothers, while the second depicts the supremacy of Joseph over the whole house of Israel. The dream of the sheaves describes Joseph's sheaf of wheat suddenly standing upright while those of his brothers gather round to do obeisance to him. It is no surprise that this causes the brothers to hate him more than before, because they were already exasperated by his cocky manners. The second dream takes in the sweep of the heavens themselves. Joseph's father and mother are the sun and moon, and the eleven stars are his brothers—the whole family is bowing to Joseph. Even his father, who had been indulgently tolerant so far, found this a bit much and scolded him (37:10).

Following the dream

There is no evidence that Joseph was even aware of the dark feelings he was stirring in his brothers' hearts. They could not see the prophetic element in his dream-sharing; because of their ill will towards him, they saw only arrogance and pride. Joseph, for his part, may have felt secure in his father's favouritism, seeing the dreams as confirmation that he would inherit, and become more important than his brothers. He may have thought that the dreams heralded the future as a foregone conclusion.

Another thing to notice is that these dreams, though obviously prophetic to us who are blessed with hindsight, did not bring Joseph any closer to God. There is no sense of awe, no worship and no thankfulness produced. Perhaps this could be put down to the enthusiasm of youth, but it illustrates a fascination with himself rather than an openness to God. Joseph was caught up in the power that the dream promised him, rather than the purpose that God had in mind for him. The prophetic cutting edge was lost to him, although not, of course, to God.

Joseph's brothers were also caught up in the power that the dream promised, and it spelled their own subjection to their upstart younger brother. Consequently a conspiracy was born and nurtured in their collective schemings, and one day it burst out in a plot to kill Joseph while he was out of his father's sight and protection. The brothers too lost sight of the prophetic dimension because they could not separate the rivalry of the years from God's signals for the future. This whole family suffered, not for lack of prophecy but for lack of prophetic awareness.

Making it personal

The challenge for us from this account of Joseph's home dreams is to hear accurately the voice of God speaking into our lives and not to get it confused with our personal story. We very often miss the voice of God because we have lost the holy art of listening. Perhaps one of our greatest needs in today's society is not a deluge of powerful charismatic gifts, nor a concentrated burst of evangelism to bring in the lost, but the simple but oh-so-necessary ability to listen. If we cannot listen, not only do we miss what God is saying but we fail to know our neighbour's story and even our own. If this is the case, we have a slim chance of knowing the love and purposes of God in our lives. It is for this reason that organizations like the Acorn Christian Foundation exist, to train people and groups in how to listen to God, to others and to themselves. Just consider for a moment the role of listening in the healing of relationships and the tough work of reconciliation. If we cannot listen to somebody else's story, no matter how much it disturbs us, then we cannot even begin to go down the road of reconciliation. Remember that the turning point for the renewal of faith in the emerging nation of Israel came when one boy, Samuel, was able to wake up to the word of God by saying 'Speak, Lord, your servant is listening' (1 Samuel 3:10).

I have been constantly astounded by the process of healing that is taking place in the ruined nation of Rwanda following its genocidal war. One of the contributors to the healing of the Hutu and Tutsi tribal relationships is Dr Rhiannon Lloyd, a paediatrician from North Wales. She invites survivors of the atrocities to tell their stories without interruption. Following this, they write their stories on pieces of paper, which they then proceed to hammer on to a makeshift wooden cross with large nails. This conveys the great truth that Jesus died on the cross in order to carry all our wounds in himself. The sacramental act of confession releases the pained and grievous feelings that the survivors carry, and the hurt and anger spills out in the group. Dr Lloyd says that it is most important that, during this time, there are people present who simply listen to these emotions in order to give respect and honour to the living and the dead. It is this cathartic climate of listening that apparently empowers these wounded people to begin the journey of forgiving their enemies. It is surely an amazing testimony to the power of God's grace and mercy that the healing of the ruined land of Rwanda is being made possible by the power of listening at the foot of the cross.

It was Dame Cicely Saunders, the founder of the Hospice Movement, who said that people will say more in a climate of listening. I think the same is true with God. If we can practise being good listeners, we may recognize his word when it comes to us, whether it is through creation, by the touch or words of others or through the still, small voice that whispers within our hearts. Or it may come through dreams and visions, which the apostle Peter said would be one of the characteristics of the coming of the Holy Spirit in these latter days of renewal (Acts 2:17). This is what it means to be truly prophetic—to listen to, acknowledge and act upon the word of the Lord when it comes to us.

A useful way to describe the dynamic process of being in touch with the prophetic realm is that we must first listen with the ears of Christ before we can speak the word of God. It is important to understand that the prime purpose of prophecy is not to tell the future but to 'forthtell' or bring the word of the Lord, the mind or perspective of God, into our lives in the here and now. We recognize this word by the fact that it carries a divine authority that demands a response from us. We can reject it or receive it, but we cannot ignore it or dismiss it. The tragedy for Joseph was that he did not recognize the prophetic word when it came. Instead of asking what the significance of the dream could be or what God was saying through it, he put himself at the centre of the dream and told his family to look at his own importance. In a way, he watered down the prophetic content so that it became a comfortable fit for his own ambitions.

We need to appreciate that the prophets were never comfortable to be the channels of God's words, as it was a costly ministry. One, Jonah, tried to run away from the prophetic call upon his life because he did not want his hated enemies, the people of Nineveh, to be blessed by it. Elijah wasted time in a cave, deluding himself into thinking that he was the only faithful witness to God, feeling all alone in his calling. Jesus summarized the story of Jerusalem as being one in which prophets were stoned and persecuted for their troubles. The coming of a prophetic word is always disturbing because it challenges us to fall under the will and ways of God—and in so doing, we give up the struggle to control and tame God, to reduce him to manageable proportions. The challenge for us is to be able to recognize the word of the Lord when it comes, to separate it out from our own agenda, and to respond to God.

Prayer

O Lord God of heaven,
birth the prophetic presence in me.
By winds and godly gale;
with the still small voice of calm;
by fire of sacred love;
in stillness and listening
sift through what is mine
so I can discover what is yours.
Teach me to dig the precious pearl of your word
out of the field of my dreams.
Amen

3

Dreams in dark places

Joseph in prison

———•◆•———

'When all goes well with you, remember me and show me kindness.'
Genesis 40:14 (NIV)

The dream

The chief cupbearer told Joseph his dream . . . 'In my dream I saw a vine in front of me, and on the vine were three branches. As soon as it budded, it blossomed, and its clusters ripened into grapes. Pharaoh's cup was in my hand, and I took the grapes, squeezed them into Pharaoh's cup and put the cup into his hand.' . . . When the chief baker saw that Joseph had given a favourable interpretation, he said to Joseph, 'I too had a dream: on my head were three baskets of bread. In the top basket were all kinds of baked goods for Pharaoh, but the birds were eating them out of the basket on my head.'
Genesis 40:9–11, 16–17 (NIV)

Both of these dreams focus on the power of the Pharaoh in the lives of two of his servants. In both dreams the cupbearer and the baker go through the motions of their normal work routines in serving Pharaoh. In a lot of dreams that we have, we are reflecting on our job and how we feel about the relationships that we have there: in the case of our two dreamers here, the all-important relationship with their employer, Pharaoh, is at the forefront. Even a casual glance at their dreams reveals the difference in mood that they contain. The cupbearer actually gets to serve Pharaoh, while the baker is thwarted in his endeavours, as his bread is picked off

16

by the birds. The story also gives us a clue that the baker is not at ease over his dream. When he hears that Joseph has given the cupbearer a favourable interpretation of his dream, the baker is desperate for a similar treatment of his own, even though he is obviously disturbed.

This reminds me of an important truth about dream work, which is that the emotions we locate *within* a dream are an important clue to their meaning. These can often be very different from how we feel *about* the dream when we awake. For example, I once worked with a doctor who had a recurring dream of failing a history exam as he sat in an old school hall. He had never failed an exam in his life, however, and at first he was amused by his dream and tempted to dismiss it as of no consequence. Yet when I asked him how he felt in the dream to be failing the history exam, his answer was, 'Utterly devastated.' He then recalled a particularly painful incident in his life which had utterly devastated him, and he saw that the dream was offering him a comment on that episode in his life. In order to understand the meaning of a dream, therefore, it can be helpful to ask ourselves if we have had the same emotion about anything going on in our waking life, either recently or some time ago. The emotions form a bridge between the dream message and the event in waking life upon which the dream may be commenting.

At the beginning of this story, both of the servants of the king want to know the meaning of their dreams (Genesis 40:8). In fact, they are sad because they do not have access to the usual resources for dream interpretation, this being an important element of belief in Egyptian society and the Middle East in general at the time.[1] The baker is more than sad, however. He is alarmed, and so he hopes for the same favourable treatment that he hears the cupbearer getting.

The story behind the dream

The two dreamers and Joseph, their interpreter, are all in prison and yet for very different reasons. The baker and cupbearer have somehow offended their master, while Joseph, though innocent, has been accused and convicted of the attempted rape of Potiphar's wife. As a reflection of their importance, Pharaoh's servants were not put into the common jail but into the house of the captain of the guard—a form of house arrest, but with certain benefits, the chief of which was to be waited upon by a servant. Joseph is in the same section of the prison, but he is there on merit and not favour. We read in Genesis 39:20–23 that after Joseph was thrown into prison the Lord was with him. As a result, the prison warden entrusted the rest of the prisoners into Joseph's care, knowing that he would keep good order. It was in this capacity that Joseph met the chief baker and the chief cupbearer.

This is a very different Joseph from the one who boasted before his brothers about his own dreams. He now seems to have acquired a servant heart, which leads him to put service for others before success in his own life The dark days of captivity, of wrongful accusation and imprisonment, have not destroyed him but, through the grace of God, have become the crucible in which the faith of a servant heart and prophetic ability have been refined in him. We can hardly escape the note of tenderness in the middle of what would have been a bleak environment. Joseph goes beyond the duties of just waiting upon people as a servant, by inquiring why they look so sad, and this leads to the whole incident of dream-sharing that we are examining.

Learning the dream message

When the cupbearer and the baker told Joseph that they had had dreams but that there was no one to interpret them, they were not telling him because they knew he had an interest or ability in dream interpretation. There is no evidence that Joseph had a growing reputation in this field and, as we saw in the last chapter, he was not a wise sharer of his own dreams, nor did he understand their true significance. Yet Joseph's reply displays that he has grown in understanding, because he says, 'Do not interpretations belong to God? Tell me your dreams' (Genesis 40:8, NIV). It is important to understand that Joseph is not saying that only God can interpret dreams. He is saying that, whatever the dreams actually mean, their significance and the message they contain come within the rule and judgment of God, who holds all our times in his hands. Joseph's words are also an indication that he is no longer going to rely totally upon his own abilities to interpret dreams, but that he needs the help of God to understand their meaning. It is this reliance upon God's help that gives his dream interpretation work such authority.

Notice that the interpretations given by Joseph obviously match the feelings and intuitions of the dreamers, because they accept the interpretations without complaint or dispute. This is a further clue as to whether we have arrived at the right interpretation of a dream: it must carry a sense of cohesion or 'right fit' with what the dreamer is feeling and sensing within the dream. There is no value in forcing an interpretation upon the dreamer; there must be a sense that it connects well and makes sense of the aspect of our lives upon which the dream is a comment.

The cupbearer is told that the three branches in the dream represent three days during which the process of budding vine to finished wine is rapidly accelerated. His dream, however, conveyed the sense of the normal routines he knew with Pharaoh, such as putting the cup of wine into his lord's hand. The mood of the dream is definitely one of restoration, and so the interpretation is a confirmation of this insight. The baker is obviously troubled by his dream. The birds of the air pick away at his bread as he goes on his way to serve Pharaoh, and so in his dream he never gets to return to his usual role within the regal household. It is a grim fulfilment of his troubled dream when he is told that the three baskets of bread also represent three days, but that at the end of those days he will be hanged and the birds of the air will eat his own flesh, and not the bread of his dream (vv. 18–19). We have an awareness that the baker is troubled by the dream because the birds' attack on his produce felt like an attack on himself.

Following the dream

Both interpretations are confirmed three days later, when Pharaoh holds a feast to celebrate his birthday and invites all his officials, including the chief cupbearer and chief baker (Genesis 40:20–22). Incidentally, although we are not explicitly told, an argument over these very preparations may well have been the reason for Pharaoh's anger with the baker and cupbearer. No actual reason is given for what happens next, but the chief cupbearer returns to his former employment and the chief baker is hanged.

Buried in the heart of this story, there is also the personal plea of Joseph. He is quite convinced that God has helped him to see the right interpretation for the chief cupbearer and that he will soon be restored to favour with Pharaoh. Therefore he says to the cupbearer, 'When all goes well with you, remember me and show me kindness; mention me to Pharaoh and get me out of this prison' (Genesis 40:14, NIV). He complains that he was forcibly carried off from his homeland and wrongly imprisoned. It is the only time that we hear Joseph opening up his heart, and here he does it with a relative stranger. He may have learned lessons of humility and dependence upon God, but not at the expense of being real and authentic. Some people have the idea that spiritual maturity is all about subduing our true self under a veneer of faith and grace. Nothing could be further from the truth. Growing in God's grace is a process of being made truly human, so that we can acknowledge to ourselves and before others those things that hurt and concern us. Spirituality is not a call to pretend that all is well. Notice the example of Jesus in the garden of Gethsemane, hours before he goes to the cross. Here is no cool, calm, collected hero marching like some Hollywood film star into the jaws of death. Jesus asks for his friends to watch and pray for him during his hours of trial. He asks his Father that, if it is possible, the cup of suffering might be taken from him. Jesus' commitment to the will of God is never in doubt; he is just being honest about how he is feeling (Matthew 26:36–46).

Joseph takes the risk of mentioning his own complaint for the first time, precisely because he knows that God is with him. Now that he has cared for another's needs, he hopes that he will in turn be cared for and rescued. He is to be bitterly disappointed. The cupbearer forgets him; his gratitude seems paper-thin and he is only interested in himself. Joseph is to remain in the prison for two more years, and no one could blame him for thinking that his dream work had been a waste of time.

Making it personal

All the servants of God must face the question at some time in their lives as to whether their work is of any value at all and whether they are in fact failures. The same thoughts would have run through Jesus' mind at his trial and execution as he remembered the days when hundreds, if not thousands, hung on his every word and marvelled at the healing miracles he did. Now he seemed quite alone. Two of his disciples followed him to the high priest's house after his arrest—Peter and another unnamed disciple (John 18:15–16).[2] Peter denied him three times, while the other was strangely silent. Nailed to the cross, Jesus' only support was a handful of women, including his mother, and John. Although disappointed in many ways, Jesus none the less kept his focus on God and on the belief that what he was doing was worthwhile— that the long-term outcome would be more beneficial than the apparent lack of immediate impact. While it is perfectly normal to want to be remembered and appreciated for the person we are and the service we give, we must embrace the fact that sometimes we will be overlooked and forgotten by the very ones we have helped. These are the times to fix our eyes on Jesus and remind ourselves that he is the cheerleader of all our gifts of service, whether we are applauded by others or entirely misunderstood.

Suffering itself is not a guaranteed way of giving us humility. It can turn us sour and bitter if we are not careful. This is why it is so important that we learn, like Jesus, to hand our complaint to God and learn to rest in the belief that God has it all in his hands, even if he does not give us satisfying insights or explanations. On the other hand, we also need to learn that just because we grow through the things we suffer, this does not mean that wrong is right. However, God is able to right wrongs through those lessons of grace and growth.

Prayer

God of the dark and difficult places,
remember me.
When forgotten, when friends are strangely silent,
remember me.
Where I wallow in the foolishness of my sins,
let me know you are there, sharing my shadows;
remember me.
While I struggle with the unfairness of things,
rage and scream,
remember me.
With my gifts unappreciated,
my work misunderstood,
remember me.
Wake my heart to see the friends I do have,
those who listen,
those with no answers,
but who know how to touch me with healing care.
So weave your light into the threads of my brokenness,
O God, and do this in remembrance of me.
Amen

4

Dreams that demand a response

Pharaoh's recurring dreams

Then Joseph said to Pharaoh, 'Pharaoh's dreams are one and the same.'   *Genesis 41:25 (NRSV)*

The dream

Pharaoh dreamed that he was standing on the bank of the River Nile. In his dream, seven fat, healthy-looking cows suddenly came up out of the river and began grazing along its bank. Then seven other cows came up from the river, but these were ugly and gaunt. These cows went over and stood beside the fat cows. Then the thin, ugly cows ate the fat ones! At this point in the dream Pharaoh woke up. Soon he fell asleep again and had a second dream. This time he saw seven heads of grain on one stalk, with every kernel well formed and plump. Then suddenly, seven more heads appeared on the stalk, but these were shrivelled and withered by the east wind. And these thin heads swallowed up the seven plump, well-formed heads! Then Pharaoh woke up again and realized it was a dream.   *Genesis 41:1–7 (NLT)*

This is the first example of a recurring dream that we have in the Bible; it is not the last, as we shall see in our chapter on King Nebuchadnezzar's two dreams. Most dream exponents tell us that recurring dreams are usually a type of nightmare and consequently have to do with some form of unfinished business in our lives. We might be threatened or challenged by something, feel unable or unwilling to deal with it and so try to deny that it is happening or forget it. This is why most nightmares end abruptly. We have simply cut the ending of the dream away before it reaches its dreadful conclusion. Yet the subject will not go away, and so some time later we dream it again, and again, until we do deal with the reality it contains. Pharaoh has two disturbing dreams, one after the other, and if they are indeed nightmares then it may just be possible that in the dream he feared that he would be the next victim of the cannibalism that both dreams contained. We are told that after the first dream, at the exact point when the thin cows devoured their healthier counterparts, the king suddenly awoke. Upon going back to sleep, he was disturbed once again, and once again stopped the dream abruptly and woke up. You cannot help but notice the feeling of relief when we are told that upon waking, 'Pharaoh realized it was a dream' (v. 7, NLT).

The other thing to notice about recurring dreams is that they normally contain the same theme, even though the symbols might be quite different between the dreams. Pharaoh dreams of cows in one dream and stalks of grain in another, and yet it is quite clear that the theme is the same. Joseph says as much when he listens to Pharaoh retelling his dreams, and says, 'Both dreams mean the same thing' (v. 25, NLT). The theme in question is the dreaded one of famine.

The story behind the dream

The story behind the dream is a very basic one—survival. The dream opens with Pharaoh standing beside the banks of the River Nile, the 'bread basket' for the nation. This fertile strip of river bank gave life to the nation of Egypt, and was so important that the symbol for the Nile delta can still be seen today adorning the walls of ancient tombs and holy places. It was in fact a symbol for life itself in the hieroglyphic script. The Nile is a regular and dependable river, fed by the heavy rains that fall on the Ethiopian highlands to the south. It swells with an annual flood from June through until October, bringing life to the virtually rainless valley and providing natural fertilizer in the form of thick volcanic silt, which the Nile has borne from thousands of miles upstream. In some places, the force of the Nile has driven back the desert for up to nine miles and for a length of over 200 miles. The Egyptians figured out how to utilize this annual flood to irrigate their valley: they planted wheat, barley and other crops in a green swathe 600 miles long. In the delta they grew vegetables, fruit, flax and grapes, and they grazed sheep, goats and cattle.

The imagery of Pharaoh standing on the banks of the Nile suggests a nation's leader inspecting the very source of his nation's sustenance and reminding himself of his source of power and wealth in the land, if not in the whole of the Middle East. This was no idle gazing on a pastoral scene but a window through which he was looking at the very survival of his kingship and people. We can begin to imagine the consternation that this dreamer felt when he saw that the land of plenty was being destroyed in such a bizarre fashion. His whole world looked as if it was about to come crashing to the ground.

Learning the dream message

The impact of the two dreams is so forceful that Pharaoh is galvanized into action to find their meaning. We are told that 'in the morning Pharaoh's mind was so troubled that he summoned all the dream-interpreters and wise men of Egypt, and told them his dreams' (Genesis 41:8, REB). This might seem strange to our ears today, as dreams do not carry the same respect and authority now as they did in ancient societies. We would hardly expect our prime minister to employ a dream interpreter on his personal staff, although President Ronald Reagan is known to have sought the advice of psychics and fortune tellers. However, this is to tar dreams with an occult brush that they do not deserve. Dreams are, as we have already seen, considered to be a respectable resource that God uses to reveal his purposes. The dream interpreters whom Pharaoh summoned were the scribes, men of priestly caste who occupied themselves with the sacred arts and sciences of Egypt, its hieroglyphic writings, the foretelling of events, and dreams. None of these learned men could interpret the dreams, however, as they proved elusive to their normal methods. These methods would have included prayer, consulting astrological calendars and taking note of any significant signs and events which had recently happened and which offered clues to the meaning of dreams. Their interpretations were arbitrary and subjective and reflected their own beliefs. Joyce Baldwin says that the failure of the scribes was because the dreams were not the usual kind, which arise out of the unconscious, but were dreams given by God directly.[1] Yet, according to Keil and Delitzsch, the dreams held definite clues in the symbols they contained, which corresponded to the religious symbols of Egypt. The cow was the symbol of Isis, the goddess of the all-sustaining earth, and in hieroglyphics it represented the earth, agriculture and food.[2] We need to realize, therefore, that no matter what insights we might have into dreams, we need the help of God in order to come to a clear understanding about the dream message, and even more so when we decide what action to take in order to follow the dream through.

With the failure of the wise men, Pharaoh is informed by his cupbearer of the successful dream interpretations given to him and the baker when they were both in prison two years earlier. Once again, the king is galvanized into action, as he is still disturbed over his dreams. 'Pharaoh sent for Joseph at once, and he was brought hastily from the dungeon. After a quick shave and a change of clothes, he went in and stood in Pharaoh's presence' (Genesis 41:14, NLT). Joseph tells the king that God will tell him what his dreams mean and that the answer will set him at ease (41:16). This does not necessarily mean that Joseph was guaranteeing a nice interpretation, as if to keep the king pacified. He was saying that the dream interpretation would exactly match and explain Pharaoh's troubled feelings and thoughts.

Then follows the time of dream sharing. It is interesting to note that Pharaoh adds some more detail to the dream in its retelling. This does not mean that he is inventing details but that he is seeing the dream more deeply as he recalls it. This is quite familiar from my years of listening to dreams: it is as if we can look with more objectivity at details that were overlooked when we were focusing more on the core of the dream. The extra details, however, often give a clue to the impact that the dream has had upon us. Pharaoh now recalls that the thin cows in the first dream were the ugliest he had ever seen in his life (41:19). He also goes on to share that, even though the thin cows ate up the fat cows, they still remained thin and emaciated (v. 21).

Tying all the threads of the dream together, Joseph informs Pharaoh that both dreams speak about a seven-year time of abundant harvest followed by seven years of devastating blight and famine. It is presented as a decree of God and not as a punishment for sin in the nation. This interpretation must have instantly explained to Pharaoh why he had been so disturbed and upset by the dream picture and so enables him to be receptive to advice about what to do in response to the dream.

Following the dream

Although he is not asked for a response to the dream message, Joseph proposes decisive action which is eminently practical and wise—a nationwide programme to collect one-fifth of the annual crop for five years and to store the excess until the times of famine come upon the nation. He even suggests that Pharaoh appoint perhaps the wisest man in Egypt to supervise the programme. There is no doubt that Joseph is taking the dream very seriously, and there is no question in his mind that it needs to be acted upon. He is not alone in his understanding of the dream's importance: Pharaoh immediately accepts the interpretation that Joseph gives. Not only this, but he also appoints Joseph to be the national co-ordinator for conserving the food and grain in Egypt. There is an old, familiar expression used in Christian circles: 'He (or she) who gets the vision usually gets the job!' So it is with Joseph: Pharaoh says, 'Since God has given you the meaning of dreams, you are the wisest man in the land! I hereby appoint you to direct this project.' (Genesis 41:39–40, NLT).

Joseph is at last lifted out of the ignominy of prison slavery and elevated to the ranks of the highest in the land. Besides being made second to Pharaoh in national policy and given rings and clothes of status, he is given a wife called Asenath, who is the daughter of Potiphera, priest of On (later called Heliopolis, the city at the southern tip of the Nile delta). Joseph's name is changed to the Egyptian one of Zaphenath-paneah, which would give him acceptance among the Egyptian hierarchy.

However, we must not be deluded into thinking that because he wore the culture of Egypt, Joseph took on its faith also. When his two children were born, even though his father-in-law was a priest of the cult of Ra, the sun god, he gave them Hebrew names to reflect his continued faith in the living God of his ancestors. Manasseh means 'made to forget', and Ephraim means 'God has made me fruitful' (41:51–52). These names form a statement of Joseph's intention to live in the present and not waste time nursing his hurts over his brothers' betrayal. They also demonstrated that he was still linked to the faith in Yahweh in which he had been cradled and raised, and which had given him his ability to work with dreams in the first place. That faith can clearly be seen when, seven years later, Joseph is confronted with his brothers bowing before him in obeisance and asking for grain to deliver them from famine and death. We are told that upon meeting them after a period of at least ten years, 'Joseph recognized them and remembered the dreams he had had many years before' (Genesis 42:9, NLT). Although it seems that he manipulated the situation to make them feel uncomfortable, by accusing them of being spies and of stealing his household gods, his aim was to bring all the brothers together—including Benjamin, the youngest son of Jacob, who was absent on the brothers' first visit to Egypt. The overall emotion, though, is not one of anger and revenge, but of pain and tears. Twice we read that Joseph broke down and wept at the sight of his brothers and seemed all too ready to forgive and embrace them in reconciliation (43:30–31; 45:1–2). He also had his sights on the long-term picture of events. He saw that despite being betrayed and sold into slavery, God had been using the situation to set in motion a series of events which would ultimately lead to the salvation and protection of his family, who would be delivered from a famine in which they would otherwise have perished (45:5–8; 50:20).

Making it personal

One of the basic truths that we must take from this account is that our dreams need to be treated with respect and acted upon in an appropriate way. Naturally, not all of our dreams are going to carry the seriousness of Pharaoh's dreams, and neither will they all be from God, but they will reflect something, however ordinary, that is of concern to us. Accordingly, it will always be good to have a trusted friend with whom you can share your dreams and perhaps pray over them. One way of helping us to locate the core issue of our dream is to ask ourselves, 'What feels like the most important thought, emotion, symbol or word in my dream?' See if this links in any way to your present or past circumstances and then make this material into something that you pray over. Then decide what might be a good and appropriate action to take, if any, to complete and fulfil the dream.

If we have been having recurring dreams, such as nightmares, where the dream ends rather abruptly, then we need to try to uncover the link issue, the repeating theme of the dreams. I have given some suggestions to help you discover these link themes in my book *Healing Dreams* and a series of taped talks entitled *Praying with Dreams* (see p. 147). It involves inviting Jesus into your dream picture, and, in the presence of a friend who listens and supports, describing the interaction of the Christ of your faith with the dream picture you have created.

This can be very cathartic and sometimes quite challenging, and so I recommend that you share the journey with someone who will be a help to you.

I had a series of recurring dreams when I was in my early 20s, in which I saw a boy of seven looking decidedly disturbed. For some reason of which I was not at first aware, I found this dream very threatening and would wake up quite suddenly from it. With a trusted friend, I retold the dream and invited Jesus simply to step into it. I then began to describe what happened next. Of course, this was a function of my own faith and perceptions, but none the less it was a valuable way to gain knowledge and a deeper understanding of myself. What I found so amazing was that, although I felt that the boy should be healed and helped to get rid of his disturbance, what unfolded in my faith-imagination work was that Jesus came and played with the little boy. It was a game of leapfrog, with Jesus as the frog. There was such laughter in the game that it took my breath away, and I began to get in touch with buried feelings of the almost total absence of play with my parents in my childhood. The dream picture had occurred over many years and had been triggered once again by the divorce of my parents after a fairly tempestuous marriage. Although I was by then an adult, the dream connected with my childhood uncertainties, which had never been properly acknowledged, let alone worked through. Jesus is the Christ of all our moments and memories, and interacting with him through a dream can be a very useful way to uncover the dream's basic link theme.

Finally, let us cultivate Joseph's long vision as we journey through life. He put his trust in God even when he was forgotten and left in prison. And at the end of his trials he was able to tell his brothers that he saw the hand of God in it all and had discovered the pattern and pathway of God's unseen preparations to save and make a mighty nation. We need the faith to believe that, no matter what darkness or frustration faces us, it is not the end of the story. God still has new and surprising chapters to write into our lives.

Prayer

When I cannot see the end of things,
when the darkness shines brighter than the sun,
when the wound will not be healed,
when I can see no answer to my questions,
when I am afraid of being hurt again,
fill me with knowing you are there, for me.
You are the first to weep over shattered lives,
the wounded healer who mends broken hearts.
The first to die and rise,
the holy victim who shouts through the silence,
'It is finished!'
When I am blinded by the power of present things,
fix my eyes on you, the battered God of the cross,
and break the power of my painful days
with reminders of new and better days still to come,
your resurrection sunrise, for me.
Amen

5

Surprised by the word of God

Eavesdropping on the enemy

———•◆•———

When Gideon heard the dream and its interpretation, he
worshipped God.   *Judges 7:15 (NIV)*

The dream

Gideon arrived just as a man was telling a friend his dream.
'I had a dream,' he was saying. 'A round loaf of barley bread
came tumbling into the Midianite camp. It struck the tent
with such force that the tent overturned and collapsed.'

Judges 7:13 (NIV)

This was a dream with two audiences—the friend of the dreamer
and a hidden enemy, Gideon, who was eavesdropping upon the
conversation and the interpretation of the dream, trying to get
up enough nerve and faith to attack the invading Midianite
army. As we shall see, the dream had dramatically different effects
on the two very different listeners, although the interpretation
was exactly the same for both of them. For the Midianite soldier,
it was chilling and unnerving and signalled his army's imminent
defeat at the hands of Israel, but for Gideon it was heart-warming
and galvanized him into action and conquest. We could well
ask, 'Who was this dream really for?' Was it only incidental for
the Midianite soldier who dreamt it, the important target for
its message being Gideon? There is a basic rule in dream work
and that is that 'the dream is for the dreamer'. What this means
is that, usually, the dream and its message are for the dreamer to
understand and to apply to his or her own life. There are some

dreams, however, which work on another level at the same time. These are prophetic dreams which carry messages for other people. An example is the dream of Pilate's wife (Matthew 27:19), which came with a message for her governor husband not to have anything to do with the condemnation of Jesus.

A quite respectful term for prophet in the Bible is 'dreamer' (Deuteronomy 13:1–5). In other words, one of the channels through which God spoke his prophetic word was dreams. 'If there is a prophet among you, I the Lord make myself known to him in a vision, I speak to him in a dream' (Numbers 12:6, RSV). As Christians, therefore, we need to stay alert to those times when God wants to speak to us through our own dreams or the dreams of others. Like any experience of God, there is no foolproof evidence to guarantee that the event is genuine and authentically from God, but as we shall soon see, there are indications that can help to confirm our faith, and then it is up to us to put our convictions into practice.

The story behind the dream

The backdrop to Gideon's eavesdropping on the enemy is a sad cycle of apostasy by the nation of Israel, and oppression and domination by an enemy tribe. In response to the nation's repentance and call to God to rescue them, a series of deliverers filled with the wild Spirit of God was raised up. Each time, the enemy was confronted and conquered, and the land and community had peace and healing; but unfortunately it only lasted during the lifetime of the deliverer. These charismatic warriors, known as 'judges', were a cross-section of people and were not necessarily the most influential or powerful in the land. Their importance lay in the fact that the Spirit of God had come upon them and given them power and authority to lead the nation into freedom and a lifestyle that was honouring to God. Earlier judges had been Othniel, the younger brother of the more famous Caleb; Ehud, who was noticeable only because he was left-handed; and Deborah, who was a prophetess. Gideon's rise to leadership came at a time when the Israelites had been under oppression for seven years.

At first sight, Gideon does not stand out as leadership material. He is introduced into the story as someone who is working furtively at night, threshing wheat in a winepress because he is afraid of being discovered. (The Midianite raids always coincided with the wheat harvest, when they overran the land and stole the crops.) Gideon works alone and apparently without his father's knowledge. Suddenly he is approached by the angel of the Lord, who salutes him with the words, 'The Lord is with you, mighty warrior' (Judges 6:12, NIV). At first we are not sure whether the angel is joking or being sarcastic. It is obvious that Gideon doubted very much if the Lord was with him, because he didn't think that he had anything to show for it. Like many of us, he asks where all the signs and wonders, proof of God's presence, have gone. Remarkably, the angel does not answer his pained questions but simply says, 'Go in the strength you have and save Israel' (Judges 6:14). Only now do we realize for sure that the angel is not joking.

When we clamour for demonstrations of power and wonder before stepping out in faith, it is often God's way to remind us of our limitations and to encourage us to commit ourselves to him for anointing. Then we can act on the belief that he will add to our smallness his great grace.

There now emerges a pattern of need in Gideon. He needs the assurance of signs before he can take steps of faith. He must have proof that God is with him before he will take risks and lead the nation to battle and the hoped-for freedom. And so he asks for three signs even before he begins the work of leadership. First there is the spontaneous outburst of fire from the rock to consume his offering of meat and bread (Judges 6:17–23) and then the two miracles concerning his fleece: the first time, only the fleece was covered in morning dew and the ground was absolutely dry, with a reversal of this sign taking place on the following day (Judges 6:36–40). It is the wonderful generosity of God that obliges Gideon even to the extent of soaking the fleece in enough dew to fill a bowl of water. There are times when God works with our need for reassurance in this kind of way, and there are times when he tests us in order to bring us to the point of recognizing and relying more upon his word of conviction than upon our need for displays of power. God now tests Gideon to see just how prepared he is to give to God rather than to receive from him.

Initially, Gideon may have taken comfort in the fact that 32,000 men had responded to his summons to war. However, God immediately focuses on where this leader's true dependence lies, by starting to reduce the number of fighting men. Gideon is guided to invite all those men who are frightened at the thought of battling with the Midianites to leave and return home (Judges 7:1–3). What a stupid thing to ask! Surely everyone would leave! I have no doubt that Gideon must have panicked at the thought of what might happen—namely the desertion of his entire army. Yet he is obedient to God, even despite these depressing thoughts about the outcome.

It is important to point out that the reason behind this apparently insane manoeuvre was not to make life miserable for Gideon (although it definitely did have this effect), but to underline the fact that *God* was going to defeat Israel's enemies, and that no victorious army was going to be able to boast in its own strength. Gideon seems to survive this shaky step of faith as he watches 22,000 fighting men go home, leaving 10,000 to face the Midianites. God has not yet finished testing him, however.

The Lord now instructs Gideon to take the troops down to the water to drink, and to select only those who drink with their fighting hand free to grab their swords should the enemy suddenly appear. The 10,000 are reduced to a mere 300 (Judges 7:6–7). We can only guess what was going through Gideon's mind as he watched his men drink and slowly realized that he had fewer seasoned fighters than he thought. Yet once again he is obedient, even though he might have been quite close to having a nervous breakdown by now! So the scene for confrontation and battle is set, and it is time to face the enemy.

Nevertheless, we still do not get the impression that Gideon is overly confident in God and in his calling to lead Israel to victory.

He is hesitant to attack a superior number who seem to have better mobility and better equipment than his army is carrying. So God invites Gideon, with his armour bearer and personal bodyguard, Purah, to go on a reconnaissance expedition in order to listen to the plans of the enemy and learn some encouraging insights. Just as Gideon is creeping up on the outposts of the camp, he overhears two friends, probably guards walking the camp perimeter, sharing a dream together. It is this eavesdropping on a stranger's dream and listening both to its content and interpretation that transforms Gideon from being a frightened leader into a dynamic conqueror.

Learning the dream message

As Gideon listens in on the dream sharing, his hope for the future, and his confidence in God to make the hope a reality, soar. The focus of the dream seems to be a cartoon or parable of what God is about to do between the tribes of Israel and the invading Midianites and Amalekites. The imagery is that of a round barley loaf tumbling into the Midianite camp, striking a tent with such force that it collapses. The interpretation is swift: 'This can be nothing other than the sword of Gideon son of Joash, the Israelite. God has given the Midianites and the whole camp into his hands' (Judges 7:14, NIV).

The symbols in this dream are actually quite important and give clues to the interpretation. The barley loaf represents the food of the poorer classes, the subsistence food of the beleaguered nation, and so would represent Israel, despised among the nations. It is also interesting that the loaf strikes 'the tent' (7:13)—not 'tent' in general but a particular tent. The accompanying sense of impending doom makes it quite likely that the tent in question belongs to the leader or general of the army, and may well house the portable gods of the tribe. In any case, for the nomad, the tent symbolizes everything associated with his power and security. The force of the loaf hitting the tent means that the interpretation of the dream as a prophetic word about Gideon and his army is quite understandable. Gideon's rise to power would have been known to the Midianites and they may have feared the implications of the popular uprising connected with his advance.

Perhaps all of this came as a shock to Gideon but one thing is for sure: he was never the same again. He exploded into action— and it was all because of a dream.

Following the dream

Gideon's response to the dream he overhears is immediate: he acknowledges the timing and purposes of God in his life. 'When Gideon heard the dream and its interpretation, he worshipped God' (Judges 7:15, NIV). Where no amount of signs and wonders affect him, the dream and its interpretation do. Why is this? The answer lies in the fact that this was not the first time that Gideon had worked with dreams to good effect. Earlier in his story we read that he had a dream in which the Lord told him to destroy his father's altar and shrine to Ba'al, the false god of the oppressing tribes. What's more, he was to take the second most important bull from his father's herd and sacrifice it to God on a new altar dedicated to Yahweh (Judges 6:25–26). Judging from what happened next, it is clear that Gideon was afraid of his father: he responds to his dream message in the dead of night, even though he has ten servants to help him (6:27). His actions bring the anger and hostility of the whole village upon him the next day, when they realize what has happened. They demand that Gideon be slaughtered for breaking down their sacred shrine. The utter surprise to Gideon is that his father stands up for him and backs his actions (6:28–32). Gideon is affirmed and recognized, and this healing of relationships ultimately leads to Gideon being filled with the Spirit of God, which testifies to the fact that his calling as the judge and battle leader of his nation has been confirmed (6:34–35).

Gideon knew the power and significance of dreams, and the overhearing of one whose origin was not in his own mind struck him with double significance. His hesitancy and fears were quickly dispelled and he was shot into action, leading to the rout of the enemy and the recovery of his nation's sovereignty. We have in this story a good example of how a dream from God strikes with authority and leads to life-changing action.

Making it personal

Discovering God's call upon us, and his guidance, comes more often when we use or give to God what little we already have, rather than simply acting in response to dramatic and super-natural interventions. This is not to deny the value of miracles, but it is to recognize that we only really step out and take risks of faith when we can put our limited selves into the hand of the invisible God. I well remember a time when I attended a mission-ary convention with my daughter Emma, when she was only seven years old. When the preacher finished his talk, he invited us all to respond to God by offering our lives afresh for his calling. We were asked to hold our hands open before us as a way of saying that we were giving to God what we were good at, and also what we were bad at, believing that he was pleased to accept both. As I was quietly praying, I felt something being placed in my hands. I opened my eyes and there was an unopened tube of fruit pastilles! I turned to my daughter, because the sweets belonged to her, and silently quizzed her as to why she had done this. She looked at me and said, 'It's all I've got. Will it do?' Mind you, an unopened tube of fruit pastilles, for a little girl, is quite a big sacrifice. It reminded me of that episode where Jesus was challenging his disciples to feed the five thousand—Andrew spotted the little boy with five loaves and two fishes and said to Jesus, in effect, 'Here are five loaves and two fishes. Can you do anything with this?' (John 6:8–9). The rest is history.

It was not the miracle of the dew-sodden fleece that sparked Gideon into following God's call to be leader of his people. He had had two dreams and they were both about affirming God's guidance for him. Both dream messages directly connected with what the angel of God had said to him, which was, 'Go in your strength.' This was not a reference to doing without the help of God, but a reminder that God would use Gideon as he was: he did not need to wait until he thought he was more fit or more powerful. All the requests for signs would only feed his need to feel powerful. The dreams underlined the fact that Gideon was called because God had chosen him as he was and not because of how he would be. It is important to remind ourselves that all Jesus' disciples were broken men. Thomas struggled with his doubts; Peter made boasts that he would defend Jesus against his enemies, and utterly failed; and James and John seemed to be controlled by their ambitious mother, Mary. But they were all called to bring their woundedness with them. Then, and only then, would they grow into wholeness through being with Jesus.

We should, therefore, cultivate an alertness to God speaking to us through our own dreams. There are a few ingredients which can help us discern when he is speaking to us in this way. Dreams from God usually carry an authority that demands a response— even if that response is to question whether God is actually speaking to us. Second, these dreams usually fit in to what God has been doing with us in our waking lives. For Gideon, it was the encounter with the angel. For Peter, it was finding himself at a crossroads in his life, when he was staying with Simon the tanner in Joppa and had his rooftop vision calling him to include the Gentiles in his witness (Acts 9:43—10:23).

This kind of dreaming comes very close to being like a vision. We create our dreams from our everyday experiences, but God can speak into them. Visions, on the other hand, are given directly by God and can occur during sleep or when wide awake. If they come during sleep they are invariably described in the Bible as 'a dream, a vision in the night' (Job 33:15; Acts 18:9), Consider, for example, how Ananias was called by God in a vision to go and pray for Saul, who was at that moment praying about his own future and also having a vision of Ananias coming and praying for his healing (Acts 9:10–16). Finally, another helpful indicator to whether the dream is from God is the simple question, 'Does this guidance conform to the revealed character and purposes of God?' One way of answering the question is to contemplate whether God will be glorified in the actions we feel called to undertake.

These pointers are, in fact, the same as the classic tests of prophecy and should give us some indication as to whether the dream is of our own making or contains a message from God. Like Gideon, we should always stay open to the God of surprises, who sometimes catches us in our sleep and gives us his calling to follow him.

Prayer

Catch me, God, in your generous grace.
Slow me down to your walking pace
so that I can see you
walking on my low roads,
standing at my crossroads.

Call me, God, with your surprising hope.
Make my ordinary life a window for wonder
so that I hear you say
'I am in love with you,
I honour and esteem you.'

Keep me, God, held in your fingers of healing.
Widen my horizons to see new possibilities
so that I know you
shining through the everyday,
dazzling me with intimacy.

Catch me, O God.
Call me, O God.
Keep me, O God.
Amen

6

Listeners make the best leaders

Samuel's wake-up call

———◆•◆———

'I'm listening,' Samuel answered. 'What do you want me
to do?'   *1 Samuel 3:10 (CEV)*

The dream

The Lord called Samuel a third time, and Samuel got up and
went to Eli and said, 'Here I am; you called me.' Then Eli
realized that the Lord was calling the boy. So Eli told Samuel,
'Go and lie down, and if he calls you, say, "Speak Lord, for your
servant is listening."' So Samuel went and lay down in his
place. The Lord came and stood there, calling as at the other
times, 'Samuel! Samuel!'   *1 Samuel 3:8–10 (NIV)*

Four times during the night, God called the boy Samuel by name.
What is not clear is whether this was part of a dream or a wake-
up call. The fact of the matter is that the call of God upon this
little boy certainly began while he slept somewhere on the temple
floor. Samuel assumed that it was the old temple priest, Eli, who
was calling him for some duty or other: after all, who else could
have been calling for him during the dark hours of the night?
There must have been some task that his mentor and trainer was
asking him to do, and we can only admire the readiness with which
Samuel responded: he ran to Eli and said, 'Here I am' (3:5–6, 8).
Samuel made only one mistake: he recognized a call or a summons
when it came, but he failed to identify the caller correctly. We are
told that the reason for this is that he did not yet know the Lord—
the word of the Lord had not yet been revealed to him (3:7). This

means that Samuel was not familiar with the ways in which God called people into prophetic mission, and he was not yet on intimate terms with his God. It was an accepted tradition that God revealed himself to prophets in visions and spoke to them in dreams (Numbers 12:6). This is what is meant by the phrase 'The word of the Lord came to . . .' a person, in, for example, Jeremiah 1:2, 4; Ezekiel 24:1 and Jonah 1:1.

Another way of describing this experience of being caught by the word of God is in the giving of visions. Compare the following examples: to Isaiah, 'The vision concerning Judah and Jerusalem' (Isaiah 1:1); to Ezekiel, 'In the thirteenth year, in the fourth month on the fifth day . . . I saw visions of God.' (Ezekiel 1:1); and to Daniel, 'I, Daniel, was troubled in spirit, and the visions that passed through my mind disturbed me' (Daniel 7:15).

This dream encounter is brief, to say the least. It consists entirely of God simply saying the name Samuel, but it is said with such conviction that, on being called the fourth time, Samuel is immediately awake and ready to hear the rest of God's message. He did not know it at the time, but this was his prophetic wake-up call, and it was going to change his life for ever.

The story behind the dream

The whole story of Samuel is a powerful contrast between those who listen to God and those who don't. His birth was an answer to prayer. Hannah, his mother, was unable to conceive and bear children and she was tormented by her rival wife, Peninnah, who held the belief that barrenness was a sign of God's disapproval. Yet Hannah did not turn bitter but poured out her pain and grief in prayer, asking God to give her a son. She even had the faith to make a vow in anticipation of getting her prayer answered: 'If you will only look upon your servant's misery and remember me, and not forget your servant but give her a son, then I will give him to the Lord for all the days of his life' (1 Samuel 1:10–11). Her persistent prayers were wonderfully answered with the birth of her son.

Hannah kept her vow and in due course brought Samuel to the temple to serve alongside the ageing priest Eli and his sons. Because Samuel's father, Elkanah, was a Levite (a descendant of Zuph, 1 Chronicles 6:26, 35), it was perfectly natural that he should work in the temple of the Lord. What is striking is that he should begin this ministry at such a young age. Levites normally began their service at the sanctuary between the ages of 25 and 50 years of age (see Numbers 8:24–25). Samuel was given to God's service after his mother had weaned him, and presumably when he was of an age to be of some basic use in the temple (1 Samuel 1:24–28). After being left in the hands of the aged priest, it is written that the boy worshipped God at the temple, and this is surely an indication of how, even though he was so young, he already had an appetite for God. Hannah's expectations were obviously that Eli would mentor Samuel, training him to become a Levitical servant to help with the maintenance and running of the temple worship. The future was to turn out very differently, however, because God had more to give to Samuel than his priestly giftings: he was going to resurrect the power of prophecy in the land through him. The stage was now set for a transformation of leadership in Israel, and more than anything else it would hinge on the ability to listen.

Samuel's boyhood time of apprenticeship contains two telling insights to his character. Three times he is described as ministering before the Lord (1 Samuel 2:11, 18; 3:1) and twice he is said to have grown up in the presence of the Lord (1 Samuel 2:21, 26). The reference to ministering is not just about Samuel carrying out the ordinary duties of looking after the upkeep of the fabric and the building. Because it is mentioned three times, it is an insight to Samuel's devotion and seeking after God. As such, he was growing in godliness all the time. The hand of God was upon him from the very beginning, and he is described as growing in favour with God and men, the very same description given of Jesus when he was a child (1 Samuel 2:26; Luke 2:52). This is no romantic description of childhood, as both Samuel and Jesus grew up in times of spiritual darkness and decay. For Samuel, the leadership and priesthood of the nation were in chaos, while Jesus was hunted like an animal from the day he was born. To remain faithful to God in times of spiritual darkness is a trial of faith, and we should take enormous encouragement from the examples of Samuel and Jesus for ourselves and for the lives of our own children.

In contrast to Samuel's determination to get close to God, we read that Eli's sons were taking God for granted and treating their priestly role as an opportunity to satisfy their own rebelliousness. Hophni and Phinehas had contempt for the routines of sacrifice that Yahweh had prescribed and were in the habit of interrupting the faithful at worship and hijacking the sacrificial offerings (1 Samuel 2:12–17). This was tantamount to a contempt for God, for their calling and for the example of their father Eli. Not only this, but they were defiling the temple by their sexual intercourse with female servants who worked at cleaning the temple entrances (1 Samuel 2:22). Although their aged father Eli complained of their behaviour and warned them of the dire consequences that God would bring upon them, he apparently did nothing to discipline them (1 Samuel 2:23–25), even when he was severely warned by prophecy of the imminent destruction that was coming upon his whole family.

The clue to the contrast is that Eli's sons do not listen to good advice when they hear it (1 Samuel 2:25). However, alongside the spiritual decline in the nation's leadership, the little boy Samuel is quietly listening out for God all the time. As we shall see, it is his capacity to listen that is to mark him out as the true leader of the nation of Israel.

The nation lay in spiritual darkness because the word of the Lord was a rare gift (3:1). The Lord had promised Israel that he would send them prophets who would make known his will and purposes at all times (Deuteronomy 18:15–16; Numbers 23:23), but the corruption in the leadership had caused this blessing to be forfeited. Yet calmly and almost unnoticed, while the spirituality of a nation was in collapse, there was Samuel, quietly waiting upon God with a listening ear. He was sleeping somewhere in the outer court and, as if to comment on the state of the nation as well as the hour, we are told that it was while the lamp of God was still lit that God first spoke to the sleeping boy (3:3). The twelve-branched lampstand was kept alight all through the night, and so we know that the time was just before dawn. We also know that, prophetically, it was just before the dawn of a renewed age when the word of God would once again be heard in the land.

Learning the dream message

We are told that the dream message consisted simply of Samuel being called by name. There are no visions or conversations to disturb him, just a voice calling him. Neither are there any details of what the call was about—no tasks given and no direction offered. It is small wonder that Samuel awakes with the conclusion that he is hearing yet another summons to do something for Eli. He learns the dream message only when Eli realizes that something unusual is going on and that the Lord is doing the calling.

Who knows what feelings must have run through the old man's mind and heart? Remember, God had hardly been speaking to anyone, and definitely not through Eli and his family. Could Eli have known that what God wanted to say to Samuel affected his own family or his ministry at the temple in Shiloh? It is a mark of the old man's grasp on reality that he knew that Samuel was, above all, a true listener, whereas his own sons were not. It is Eli who gives the boy the key to understanding what is going on and instructs him that when he is next called, he must respond simply by saying, 'I'm listening, what do you want me to do?' (1 Samuel 3:9, CEV).

God comes to Samuel a fourth time, and there is such intimacy in the way that this is described: 'The Lord came and stood there' (1 Samuel 3:10, NIV). This seems to confirm that although Samuel is initially called when he is asleep, God intends to wake him up before identifying the nature of his calling. Samuel invites God to speak, and he is told a disturbing prophecy: God is about to do something that will affect the whole nation, and it will involve the destruction of Eli's family. It is going to be something so startling and disturbing that it will 'make the ears of everyone who hears it tingle' (1 Samuel 3:11, NIV). Samuel is not told what the catastrophe is going to be, and the only detailed part of the prophecy is to do with Eli's family.

We may wonder why God first spoke to Samuel while he was sleeping. In my work with dreams and sleep, I have come to the conclusion that we are more honest with ourselves when we are asleep, because we seem to be more in touch with what we are feeling, thinking and perceiving. In waking life, we repress many things that disturb us or do not fit into our scheme of things. Often, the issues with which we have been unconsciously wrestling or debating are given space to be faced and worked through. This has been proved true, for example, in the field of scientific endeavour. Friedrich Kekulé, who laid the foundations of organic chemistry with his discovery that carbon atoms link together in rings, testified to achieving a breakthrough in his research as a result of a dream. Kekulé wrote about his chemical researches at a time when they were not going too well:

> I turned my chair toward the fireplace and sank into a half sleep. The atoms flitted before my eyes ... wriggling and turning like snakes. One of the snakes seized its own tail and the image whirled scornfully before my eyes. As though from a flash of lightning I awoke; I occupied the rest of the night in working out the consequences of the hypothesis. Let us learn to dream, gentlemen![1]

If, while we are asleep, we are so much more open or honest to the life issues that we carry within us, it is no surprise that God should choose such moments to speak to us and get our attention.

Following the dream

Surprisingly, Samuel went back to sleep after his disturbing encounter with God. Next morning, he is afraid to upset Eli with the news of his family's imminent destruction. He recognizes that the sharing of prophecy is not always an easy and never a casual affair. Eli is fully aware that Samuel is avoiding him, because he too must have wondered through the night what had happened. Consequently, Eli has to seek him out and gently encourage him to tell all, by beginning the conversation with the words, 'Samuel, my son . . .' (1 Samuel 3:16). He strongly urges the boy to share fully what God has said to him, and so Samuel gives him the bad news. Eli had already been warned through prophecy of this terrible news (2:32, 34) and he calmly acknowledges that the prophetic word is true. It not only corroborates what God has already been doing in his life but obviously comes with all the authority that divine prophecy usually carries.

This listening to and giving of God's word marks the turning point in Samuel's life. From now on he is described as a prophet of the Lord (1 Samuel 3:20) and we learn that the word of the Lord is now being communicated to him and through him throughout the land. As we have already seen, one of the ways in which God communicates his word is through dreams and visions. Samuel had been launched into his new ministry, and his position of authority would affect the whole nation for the rest of his life. We must remind ourselves, however, that his calling to be a channel for the word of God hinged on his ability and appetite to listen to God when all others had long abandoned their interest in doing so.

Making it personal

I was struck by an advertisement I saw in *The Times* concerning the need for accurate telecommunications. It was a picture of the huge statue of Abraham Lincoln in Washington DC. Sitting astride the giant shoulders of the great man was a cleaner, who was in the process of scrubbing the ears on the statue. The punchline underneath read, 'Listeners make the best leaders.' If anyone in the Bible demonstrated this truth, it was Samuel. He alone knew how to listen to God accurately, and because he did so he heard the word of the Lord for his day and age. We too must learn to listen not just to God but to others and to ourselves. As you think of the spiritual crisis facing the Church and nation of our day, what do you look for as the means of challenging and changing the situation? A mighty evangelist? A summons to prayer that we might call upon God to heal our land? Or an outpouring of the Holy Spirit which will sweep away sin and evil? Let us learn from Samuel's experience and look for listeners who listen with the ears of Christ so that they can be empowered to speak the word of God.

I have always been impressed with that Servant Song in Isaiah which describes the gifts and training of the true servant of the Lord: 'The Sovereign Lord has given me an instructed tongue, to know the word that sustains the weary. He wakens me morning by morning, wakens my ear to listen like one being taught' (Isaiah 50:4, NIV). If we want to be in touch with God's will and purposes for ourselves and our nation, we must cultivate, above all others, the gift of listening. This will save us from being people of many and any words, and enable us to become people with 'the word that sustains the weary'. We will be those who have the word for our times—and it is this sure word of God that needs to be on the lips of all proclaimers, giving true direction to our praying, and preparing us for those surprising and longed-for times when God pours out his Spirit on a people ready to receive him.

Prayer

In stillness,
like the early morning air before the birds awake to dawning light;
in tempests,
when I am tossed by the rage of voices within and about;
teach me to listen
and discover your word to match my need.

For the broken and the brittle,
for the confused and the cornered,
for those who struggle to find the straight path;
teach me to listen
so that they might discover your careful cradling.
Amen

7

Becoming a wise one
Solomon's dream interview

———◆◆◆———

Then Solomon awoke—and he realized it had been a dream.
1 Kings 3:15 (NIV)

The dream

At Gibeon the Lord appeared to Solomon during the night
in a dream, and God said, 'Ask for whatever you want me to
give you.' Solomon answered, 'You have shown great kindness
to your servant, my father David, because he was faithful to
you and righteous and upright in heart. You have continued
this great kindness to him and have given him a son to sit
on his throne this very day. Now, O Lord my God, you have
made your servant king in place of my father David. But
I am only a little child and do not know how to carry out
my duties. Your servant is here among the people you have
chosen, a great people, too numerous to count or number.
So give your servant a discerning heart to govern your people
and to distinguish between right and wrong. For who is able
to govern this great people of yours?'

The Lord was pleased that Solomon had asked for this.
So God said to him, 'Since you have asked for this and not
for long life or wealth for yourself, nor have asked for the
death of your enemies but for discernment in administering
justice, I will do what you have asked. I will give you a wise
and discerning heart, so that there will never have been anyone like you, nor will there ever be. Moreover, I will give you
what you have not asked for—both riches and honour—so

that in your lifetime you will have no equal among kings. And if you walk in my ways and obey my statutes and commands as David your father did, I will give you a long life.' Then Solomon awoke—and he realized it had been a dream.

1 Kings 3:5–15 (NIV)

This is perhaps the longest dream narrative in the Bible, and it takes the form of a dialogue between the recently crowned king and Yahweh. Solomon has come to worship and offer an extravagant 1000 burnt offerings to God in celebration and thanksgiving for the beginning of his reign as David's successor on the throne of Israel. The dream is basically a conversation which God himself initiates, and it is very detailed in its content.

Dreams including lengthy conversations are not so very unusual when you examine the range of dream material that people describe. Two pioneers in this field, Nathaniel Kleitman and Eugene Asherinsky, made a breakthrough in dream exploration in 1952, when they discovered what is now popularly described as 'rapid eye movement' or 'REM'. This occurs approximately six or seven times during an average sleep cycle and is a period during which the eyes move rapidly from side to side, as if the sleeper is watching a fast-moving film. It is basic to the laws of sleep, and even people blind from birth have periods of REM, although the content of their dreams does not include visual images. Eighty per cent of people awakened during REM sleep are able to record vivid and detailed dream material; it seems that we are now able to locate the more detailed dreaming moments of our sleep. REM sleep lasts for a few minutes on average, but people's descriptions of the dreams they have during this time last a lot longer than the REM period itself. Another important factor in dream experience is that the brain is just as active when we are asleep as when we are awake. According to William Dement, 'EEG [electroencephalography] shows that the neurones in the brain are amazingly active, as if the brain were living the dream while encased in its motionless body.'[1]

We can conclude from this brief research into REM sleep that if the brain is so engaged while we sleep, it must be perfectly possible for the sleeper to have as meaningful a 'conversation' as when he or she is awake. I am reminded of the words of the beloved in the Song of Songs: 'I slept but my heart was awake' (Song of Songs 5:2). In Hebrew psychology, human nature is a unity of spirit, thought and emotions, so the word for 'heart' (*leb*) means the conscious self. The beloved is asleep but her thoughts and longings are for her absent suitor, and in her dreams she goes on calling out for him. Solomon is asleep but his thoughts are full of recent events, and into these nocturnal deliberations steps God to speak to the sleeping king about his needs. Unlike his approach to the boy Samuel, God does not want to wake up the dreamer; this time he wants to conduct an interview with Solomon in his sleep, and it is just as valid as if the king was standing awake before him. The reasons are fairly obvious: Solomon had a lot on his mind when he went to lie down. This being so, God is perfectly able to pick up the thread of Solomon's concerns and weave his purposes into them. Solomon is about to discover just how effective this dream interview is to prove.

The story behind the dream

Solomon did not come peacefully to his coronation. If anything, it was a rushed job. The dark shadow over the event was an attempted coup in the palace. His father David was now very old and losing his hold on reality as well as on his throne. Such times of weakness are often shrouded by intrigue among those who see an opportunity to seize power for themselves. It was well known that David had promised the succession to his young son Solomon (1 Kings 1:13, 17, 30), but his oldest surviving son, Adonijah, was not going to take this lying down, and so he grabbed the moment of opportunity. He gathered support from Joab, the leading general of the Israelite army, and Abiathar, the high priest for the nation, and together these conspirators went to the high place of Zoheleth, where Adonijah made sacrifices to God and had himself crowned king. Adonijah must have felt very confident, because he invited along the rest of his brothers (excluding his rival Solomon) and as many royal officials as were in sympathy with his claim to be king (1 Kings 1:7–10). Inevitably the next step would be the wholesale slaughter of his rivals, including, no doubt, Solomon himself and all government officers and army staff. The situation looked very desperate indeed.

It was the quick thinking of Nathan, the royal prophet, that saved the day. He was probably also marked for death by Adonijah, but as soon as he heard the alarming news he informed Bathsheba, David's favourite wife and the mother of Solomon. Together they hurriedly told David what was happening. The old king must have remembered the former coup under his other son, Absalom, and knew what was coming if he did not act swiftly. He gave orders that Solomon was to be consecrated king at Gihon with all the formalities, which included riding on the king's donkey and being anointed by Zadok the priest, with oil taken from the 'sacred tent' in Jerusalem. The ceremony was to be attended by the palace bodyguards and completed with a celebratory procession back into the city of Jerusalem (1 Kings 1:32–45). Both Solomon's and Adonijah's celebrations were held in close proximity to each other, which is why Adonijah overheard the trumpet blowing and rejoicing over Solomon's anointing as king. Zoheleth was in a shady part of the valley of Hinnom, while Gihon was on the opposite, western side of the same valley, less than 700 yards from the city walls. The intention was to send a signal to the camp of Adonijah that an authentic and proper coronation had taken place. It had the desired effect, because the camp of conspirators fell into disarray and Adonijah dashed to the tabernacle to seek sanctuary. He was allowed to live under a form of house arrest as long as he behaved himself. This he did—but he was biding his time, waiting for another window of opportunity to seize the crown. It was not long in coming.

Not long afterwards, David died and Adonijah asked permission to marry Abishag, the king's favourite concubine. This was no less than an attempt to legitimize his claim to the throne. It was recognized at the time that to take over the deceased king's harem was to establish a claim to the throne (2 Samuel 12:8; 16:21).

Solomon recognized the plot immediately and once again swift action was necessary. Adonijah was executed for his intrigue, along with Joab, his fellow schemer (1 Kings 2:13–25, 28–29).

Now that all Solomon's enemies had been vanquished and the crown was firmly in his hands, the time had come to rule confidently. He made an alliance with Egypt by marrying Pharaoh's daughter, and thought about building the temple in Jerusalem, which had been the last commission of his father (1 Kings 3:1–3). Yet he still did not feel overconfident in his rule—he was only about 20 years old, after all. So he went to another high place, Gibeon, to offer more sacrifices and to get ready to rule over a nation so recently divided by civil distress. As he went to bed that night, he would have had a lot on his mind and much to mull over as he thought about the future.

Learning the dream message

Solomon's dream message is a summons and an interview. God offers the young king a blank cheque: he will grant him whatever he wants. It is an insight to the king's heart that, above all other things, he wants to be wise. He is honest about his limitations and the size of the task before him. He feels like a child, but has the business of leading a strong nation, so he asks for discernment so that he can govern wisely a people who, after all, belong to God. Solomon is also aware of the debt he owes to David, who handed over to him such a strong kingdom. He knows, however, that David's kingdom is strong precisely because David was faithful to God and kept his integrity. Solomon recognized a good mentor when he saw one, and wanted to learn from this and lead his people equally well.

God is pleased with this request because essentially it is not selfish. Instead of asking for the death of his enemies, or success, or long life in order to increase his hold on power, the king's focus is on the nation's need for wise leadership. Therefore, God grants Solomon his first request for wisdom and much more besides. He promises him wealth and honour and the deep-seated concern of his heart, which had perhaps been unspoken in this interview—security upon the throne. This security will not come through having power over enemies but by walking in the ways of the Lord (1 Kings 3:10–14).

Following the dream

There is almost a note of surprise in the description of how Solomon awoke in the morning and suddenly realized that the divine interview that had just taken place in fact happened in a dream (3:15). This is a telling insight into just how profound the experience had been for him. He certainly did not dismiss it as 'only a dream', and this reveals the respect and importance accorded to dreams by people in Old Testament times, and the belief that they could contain valuable insights to the ways and words of God. Solomon's response was not to dismiss the whole thing as wishful thinking and give it no credence. On the contrary, it gave him the faith and energy he was hoping for, to lead his people as effectively as David had done. His immediate reaction was to return to Jerusalem, a short distance away, and perform three important acts of faith (3:15). First, he stood before the ark of the Lord's covenant in its temporary headquarters in the sacred tent in the city. This was the ark before which Moses and Joshua had communed with God as they battled their way across the desert to the land of promise. This was the ark before which David had danced when he rescued it from the hands of the Philistines and brought it home to the heart of the community of Israel (2 Samuel 6:14–15). It spoke of the faithfulness of God to keep covenant with his people and always be present among them. Who knows what private thoughts and prayer passed through Solomon's mind that day? He would at least have been dedicating his life to be the leader that God had called and gifted him to be. He would have been seeking to deepen his intimacy with the God who had stepped into his dreams, promising to support him as long as he walked in the ways of his father David.

Second, Solomon made sacrifices of burnt and fellowship offerings. 'Burnt offerings' was a general term covering the sacrifices performed for those seeking forgiveness and renewal of their heart with God. The king knew his limitations and had to tell God that he needed him and his help for the challenging days that lay ahead. Lastly, the king threw a celebration for all his court. He was now showing thankfulness for their support, because he would continue to need it. The king wanted to celebrate and to give thanks with his friends. It is a lonely person who feels that their walk with God is a totally private affair, not to be shared with friends.

We could say that the rest is history. There is the well-known story of the two prostitutes claiming to be the mother of the same child, and Solomon's wisdom in finding the true mother by preparing to cut the child into two pieces. The real mother protested and offered to give her child to the rival claimant, in order to save the life of the child she truly loved. She was given back her son alive and well (1 Kings 3:16–28). Solomon's fame as a wise man spread beyond the borders of his own nation, and people came from all over the East to listen to what he had learned. He went on to build the temple of the Lord and indeed met with God once again, in another dream at Gibeon, on the eve of its consecration (1 Kings 9:1–9). There is abundant evidence that the dream interview had sparked him into the reality of wise living and leadership that God had promised him. For as long as he lived out the message of his dream, Solomon would lack no support from his Lord and he need never look back in fear.

Making it personal

The first thing to learn from Solomon's experience is the priceless gift of wisdom. It will save us from so much heartache and ruin. How often I have regretted saying things without first thinking over them with God. I have made judgments on people, only to learn later that I did not know the whole story or all the factors surrounding the event. The effect of my unkind words could not be taken back, only repented of, but sometimes much damage has been done.

I remember being asked, as a young assistant minister at a Baptist church on the Wirral, if I would visit someone who had formerly attended our church. I was told that unfortunately she had married the local bookmaker, who was not a Christian, and that he had taken her away from the Lord. Could I go and witness to them and encourage the wife to come back to the fold? So off I went with the zeal to rescue her in my heart and was greeted at the door by the non-Christian husband. 'I suppose you have come to try and save me?' he questioned. I steeled my heart against the adversary! However, he completely baffled me when he said later that he had wanted so much to become a Christian and had even upset his father by walking out on the bookmaking business to go and do something more useful with his life. I asked him to tell me his story. He shared how he had gone to South Africa before he was married, and hoped to begin a new life. He found himself walking past an evangelistic meeting being held in a large tent. As he read the noticeboard outside the tent, he was suddenly accosted by a very large man, who turned out to be the evangelist. He was brought into the meeting rather reluctantly and was horrified when the evangelist commanded him to kneel at the front of the tent. He did this, more out of fear than conviction. Grabbing the microphone, the speaker prayed over him as if he had come to find salvation and forgiveness. There had been no conversation and certainly no respect for his dignity. The man told me that he had felt sickened and abused by the whole experience, and that it had put him off Christianity, so he had meekly returned to running his father's bookmaking business. I could only apologize for what this other Christian had done. Wonderfully, this opened the way to our becoming friends, and he became much more open to looking into his desire for faith again. It taught me the lesson of never making judgments if possible, and always seeking to listen to and learn the whole story before acting. Wisdom is so important that it is listed as a charismatic gift in the New Testament (1 Corinthians 12:8) and

I think that it is all about offering our beliefs to others at the right time and in an appropriate manner.

The greatest insight that Solomon received through his dream interview was that God cared for him just as much as he had cared for his father David. Jesus sought to impress this love of God upon his disciples and friends over and over again. He constantly described God as his own father and their father, and even taught them a prayer that began, 'Our Father . . .' (Matthew 6:9). And so he encourages us not to worry unduly because, above and beyond all that could happen to us, God is still there, loving us. Jesus points to how the birds are fed and how the flowers bloom in more glory than the whole of Solomon's court, because God cares for the whole of his creation and for us in both our crises and our ordinary times. Whatever our circumstances, whether we are in the dark of indecision or riding high on our successes, nothing alters the deeper, simpler and profounder truth that God loves us with a passion.

Prayer

Make me a wise one, O Lord,
who knows how to see through the appearance of things,
and hold on to what is good.
Make me a wise one, O Lord,
who sees better days coming for the walking wounded.
Put me into your places where I
breathe heart into the fallen,
birth new life into the discouraged,
bring your good word to the crushed,
buy time for the desperate.
Make me a wise one, O Lord.
Amen

8

Interlude

The therapy of dreams

——•◆•——

> God always answers, one way or another, even when people
> don't recognize his presence. In a dream, for instance, a vision
> at night, when men and women are deep in sleep, fast asleep
> in their beds—God opens their ears and impresses them with
> warnings, to turn them back from something bad they're
> planning, from some reckless choice, and keep them from
> an early grave, from the river of no return.
>
> *Job 33:14–18 (The Message)*

This passage forms part of the counselling advice given to Job
as he battles with appalling suffering, having witnessed the
destruction of almost his entire family and the loss of his business empire. Neither he nor his three friends have any idea of
the dialogue in the heavenly realm between God and Satan, in
which God gave permission to Satan to test Job to the uttermost
but not to take his life (Job 1:1—2:10). They are joined by a
fourth person called Elihu, who waits until the first three
friends have exhausted their theology and advice (32:1–5).
Apparently Elihu's sole motivation is to uphold the righteousness of God because Job seems to be seriously doubting if
God really cares for him at all. Job cannot understand why God
is silent, and he longs to hear a word from the Lord. Elihu sets
about trying to convince Job that God does care and does act
on our behalf. He points out that one of the ways in which
God still speaks is through dreams and visions. There are, in
fact, four reasons why God gives dreams and visions, according
to Elihu:

- to give us warnings
- to offer guidance
- to provide spiritual discipline
- to lead to salvation.

To give us warnings

> He makes them listen to what he says, and they are frightened
> at his warnings.   *Job 33:16 (GNB)*

Perhaps the best collection of warning dreams in the Bible is the group connected with the birth of Jesus (Matthew 2). There seems to be a veritable outpouring of warning dreams at this time. Joseph and Mary are warned to flee the wrath of King Herod, who was determined to kill the baby before he became the King of kings who would menace his dynasty. When they later return from the refugee life in Egypt, they are warned again to live in the relatively safe district of Nazareth, where they can be anonymous. The Magi are warned to get out of the country as quickly as they can, avoiding all contact with Herod, and they subsequently disappear from the story as quickly as they entered it.

Now, the whole point of a warning dream is to get our attention. The way that God got the attention he required was by using direct speech spoken with urgency and compelling authority. When we want to warn someone of imminent danger, we speak up or even shout at them, and no doubt upset them—but we get their attention. If a little child was chasing a football into the face of oncoming traffic, the last thing you would do is to go into your house in search of the Green Cross Code to teach the child kerb drill. No, you would scream with as much power and alarm as you could muster and say, 'Stop!' The child may be alarmed to hear you scream, but you will get his or her attention and the danger will be avoided.

We may have dreams that upset us and disturb us, but we must resist the temptation to conclude all too quickly that they are bad dreams and try to forget them. They may well be warning dreams that need to be heard and worked through. One of the things we need to appreciate is that warning dreams use exaggeration to get us to listen and look at the message. Take the example of a woman who had a series of recurring dreams in which she repeatedly fell down her stairs at home. At the beginning, the dream showed her tripping over a hole in her stair carpet and falling down. As the dreams progressed, she tripped over the hole and fell down what seemed like an endless flight of stairs. She was finally stirred into action when she dreamed again of tripping over but this time, as she fell down the stairs they opened up like a set of crocodile teeth and swallowed her up. She was quite frightened by this later development and so shared it with someone who could help her understand her dream. As she was a member of a church that focused on spiritual warfare, she wondered if the dream was a symbol of Satan as the great dragon who was seeking to devour her because she was a Christian. Her friend asked her if she had a hole in her stair carpet. She answered, 'Yes, but what's that got to do with it?' She explained that her stair carpet did in fact have a hole in it, and she had been meaning to change it for some time but kept putting it off. It now became clear that because she was not paying sufficient attention to what was happening in waking life, her dreams sought to find a way to bring her attention to something she was avoiding! We too must learn to listen accurately to our dreams and explore if we are receiving some warning from them.

To offer guidance

> God does speak . . . to turn man from wrongdoing.
>
> *Job 33:14, 17 (NIV)*

God is so in love with us that he tries to heal us before we make decisions that will make our lives sick. Consider the remarkable dream of King Abimelech of Gerar, who had forcibly taken Abraham's wife Sarah and intended to add her to his harem (Genesis 20:3–7). Before he had had intercourse with her, however, he was rudely confronted by God in his dream, who said to him, 'You are as good as dead because of the woman you have taken; she is a married woman.' Abraham had been convinced that Abimelech would kill him if he knew that Sarah was his wife, and so together they had deceived him into thinking that she was only his sister—a half-truth because Sarah was, in fact, Abraham's half-sister (Genesis 20:12). God alerted the king to the truth of the matter; he swiftly returned Sarah to her husband and a disaster was averted.

In the New Testament, a good example of a warning dream is the conversion of the apostle Paul at the time when he was a zealot, bent on destroying the newly emerging band of Christians. His encounter with God's preventative medicine came on the Damascus road. In what later he described as 'the heavenly vision' (Acts 26:19), he was faced by God, who seemed to speak right through his mask of pious zeal to the troubled Pharisee who was looking for intimacy with God. This accounts for Paul's rapid acknowledgment of and submission to Jesus when God instructed him to wait for his proper calling—to build up the body of Christ and not to break it down (Acts 9:1–6). Paul was turned from a path that began when he was a willing bystander to the martyrdom of Stephen and threatened to end in an orgy of violence in Damascus. Paul's experience came through a day-time vision but, as we shall see later, dreams and visions are very similar experiences in the Bible.

To provide spiritual discipline

God does speak . . . to keep him from pride.

Job 33:14, 17 (NIV)

With these words, Elihu may have been trying to suggest to Job that the torments he was enduring were God's way of challenging his pride and bringing him into a humility he badly required. I think Elihu is way off the mark here, for despite all his outbursts, Job is actually commended by God for keeping his integrity (Job 42:7). This is not to deny, however, that dreams can become the place where God challenges our self-centredness and damaged pride. As we shall see in more detail later, the whole thrust of the vision or waking dream that Peter had on the rooftop in Joppa was about his spiritual and national pride. God was challenging him to wake up to it and see further than his own limited vision of ministry. He was to swing the door wide open so that the Gentiles could come pouring into the kingdom of God and become joint members of the Church of Christ (Acts 10:9–23).

I remember having a dream shortly after my very first book *Dreams and Spirituality* had been published by Grove (1985). I had eagerly gone down to my local Christian bookshop in Leicester to see it on the shelves and hopefully to see people buying it. However, I had great difficulty in locating it myself! This was because, being a Grove book, the title did not appear on the spine, and so I had to hunt to find it. When no one was looking, I took the copies off the shelves and replaced them face out, so that others could plainly see them. Yet on subsequent visits to the shop, I found that a staff member had come along and tidied my books away so that they were almost lost in the general crowd of titles. I am sorry to confess that I played this cat-and-mouse game for some weeks before realizing that there was not a lot of interest in my book. It was following this that I had my dream. In it, I was standing by a huge bonfire of burning books, rather like my impressions from the 1930s newsreels of the burning of the books at the infamous Reichstag fires in Nazi Germany. It was not copies of books written by 'undesirables' that were burning, however. The fire consisted totally of my book going up in flames. Standing next to me was a man who looked like a monk or a holy person, and so I turned to him and said something like, 'It's not fair. They're burning all my books.' The wise old monk turned to me and said, 'That's because of your pride! You are more interested in selling them than really caring for people.' It came as a jolt and it woke me from my sleep. I realized at once the truth of the dream message: I was indeed, like a lot of writers, unduly concerned to be a success and not paying attention to the needs of others. I recognized that God had spoken a truth to me and I have tried to learn from it ever since.

To lead to salvation

> God opens their ears ... to keep them from an early grave, from
> the river of no return.   *Job 33:18 (The Message)*

The NIV translates verse 18 as 'to preserve his soul from the pit, his life from perishing by the sword'. This is an act of saving grace if ever there was one! The basic word for 'salvation' in the New Testament, *soteria*, has a number of meanings. It can mean to be delivered from danger and apprehension, as in being saved from our enemies (Luke 1:71), or from drowning at sea, as in the case of Paul's shipwreck on the way to Rome (Acts 27:34). It can also be used in a spiritual sense, as in those who put their trust in Jesus Christ and are delivered from the punishment for their sins (Romans 10:10; Ephesians 1:13). Finally, it can refer to being delivered from the actual bondage of sin (Philippians 2:12). Paul had a dream vision when he was on his way back through northern Turkey, en route to his church base in Palestine. He records being blocked by the Holy Spirit from going in a certain direction and then, one night in the middle of this challenging time, dreaming of a man in Macedonia crying out for help. Paul saw this as God's direction for him to take the message of the gospel into Europe, which was not his plan at the time. Because he was obedient, however, the gospel of salvation was brought into a new territory where the church was to grow strong and rapidly (Acts 16:6–10).

We can conclude from this brief introduction that God puts an enormous value on dreams and visions as a vehicle for communicating his guidance into our lives and circumstances. There are also indications in the Bible that the ability to understand and work with dreams is a resource for ministry.

Dreams and prophecy

As we have noted already, in the Bible a prophet is respectfully called a 'dreamer' (Deuteronomy 13:1–5), because a prophet was known to hear God's word through visions and dreams

(Numbers 12:6). Many were called through visionary experiences, such as Moses with his vision beside the burning bush (Exodus 3:1–3). Ezekiel was called to his work through a vision of God seated on his chariot throne (Ezekiel 1), and throughout his life his ministry was characterized by similar visual unveilings of the spiritual condition of Israel and its future destiny (Ezekiel 10:1–22; 37:1–14) Daniel was sometimes overcome by the visions that unfolded before him, to do with the deliverance of nations (Daniel 7:1–14; 8:1–14). John, struggling with the prison regime on the island of Patmos, receives a catalogue of revelations pointing to the climax of the ages (Revelation 1:9–20; 21:1—22:6).

Dreams were so important a way of hearing God's voice that the lack of them drove King Saul into a pathetic attempt to get God's guidance through consulting the witch of Endor (1 Samuel 28:6–7).

A prophet was known as one who saw beyond the appearance of things to connect with the word of God. The early name for prophet was 'seer', meaning 'one who sees beyond or above'. Interestingly enough, the Hebrew word for 'vision' is *hardzar*, implying the ability to see with the inner eye. The same meaning is found in the New Testament words for visions, which are *onar* (Matthew 1:20; 2:12; 27:19), *horama* (Matthew 17:9; Acts 7:31, 56; 10:3) and *optasia* (Luke 1:22; 2 Corinthians 12:1). In other words, prophets are open to 'seeing' the word of God come to them in both ordinary and extraordinary forms—as dreams and visions are essentially to do with a capacity for 'seeing', it is no wonder that this is one of the chief methods that God uses.

Dreams and spiritual wisdom

We have already explored the Joseph dream stories and seen how his ability to interpret dreams was accepted as a sign of his being a wise man on whom rested the wisdom of God. One of the reasons why Joseph was elevated so rapidly to high office was because his wisdom was more powerful than that of the court officials. A very similar experience befell Daniel, who was a prisoner in exile. In preparing him for service in captivity, we are told that God particularly gifted Daniel with the understanding of visions and dreams of all kinds (Daniel 1:17). Sadly, in the West, we seem to have lost almost all our respect for dreams, as we have become a more scientifically based society, mistrusting the validity of the intuitive and the supernatural. It is a subject relegated to the fringe—the not-so-orthodox in our world. We need to repent of our lack of faith and ask God to renew our respect for his ability to speak into and through our dreams, and to give us visions whether in our sleep or when we are wide awake.

Dreams and personal renewal

On the day of Pentecost, with the Holy Spirit poured out upon him, the apostle Peter stood up and described this event, with its manifestations of speaking in tongues and prophesying, as a fulfilment of the prophecy of Joel (2:28–32; see Acts 2:16). According to this prophecy, some of the signs of the last days would be as follows: 'I will pour out my spirit on all people. Your sons and daughters will prophesy, your old men will dream dreams, your young men will see visions.' We must not be tempted to see the reference to 'old men' as a reference to mindless daydreaming by those who have had their day. The Greek word that Peter used for old men is *presbuteroi*, which we translate as 'elders' or 'bishops', while the Hebrew word in Joel refers to those who are zealous for God, and is sometimes explained as those who are experienced pioneers in the field of faith and exploits. These are men in their spiritual prime, hearing the word of God in their dreams. Dreams and visions are channels for God to effect his renewal in our personal lives and ministries. They offer another way of being open to heaven's initiatives as we work to bring the kingdom of God closer to our society, in the power of the Holy Spirit.

We can conclude, therefore, that dreams are of great significance in the ways that God works, and ignoring or dismissing them diminishes our awareness of God in our lives. Dreams are also our own personal journey of discovery in which we explore what is going on in and around our lives. If we listen to our dreams, we can discover more of who we are and open more of ourselves to the fresh winds of God's renewal in our lives.

Prayer

Wild Spirit of the living God,
make a dreamer out of me.
Step into my sleep
and call me to new adventures on the tides of your turning grace.
Let my night times
be charged and changed with the dawning day of new insights.
Let my resting in the dark
lead to dancing in the blazing morning of new revelations
of the depths and the layers of your care for the whole of me,
sleeping and awake.
Let the ending of the day
lead to glimpses of one like the son of man
whose face is like the sun shining in all its brilliance.
Amen

9

Seeing the end of all things

Nebuchadnezzar's dream of a multi-metalled man

———◦◦◦———

'The great God has shown your majesty what will happen
in the future.'   *Daniel 2:45 (NLT)*

The dream

(Daniel said) . . . 'While your majesty was sleeping, you dreamed
about coming events . . . in your vision you saw in front of
you a huge and powerful statue of a man, shining brilliantly,
frightening and awesome. The head of the statue was made
of fine gold, its chest and arms were of silver, its belly and
thighs were a combination of iron and clay. But as you watched,
a rock was cut from a mountain by supernatural means. It
struck the feet of iron and clay, smashing them to bits. The
whole statue collapsed into a heap of iron, clay, bronze, silver
and gold. The pieces were crushed as small as chaff on a
threshing floor, and the wind blew them all away without
a trace. But the rock that knocked the statue down became
a great mountain that covered the whole earth.

Daniel 2:29–35 (NLT)

This was an extremely disturbing dream for a king and despot to
have. For reasons that he did not at first understand, Nebuchadnezzar was so troubled by his dream that he elected not to tell
it to anyone. This was not because he wanted to forget the dream
but because he wanted to wait until he could find somebody who
was authentically in touch with his dream and, more importantly,
its interpretation. He was desperate to know that he was going to

get the right interpretation of his dream and not one that appealed to the interpreter's own science or philosophy.

There is a famous apocryphal story based on the fact that Freud and Jung used to share their dreams with each other, with Freud usually doing the interpreting and Jung the sharing. On one occasion, Jung declared to Freud that he had dreamt of holding two eggs in his hands. Freud, as many know, had developed a theory of sexuality and symbols with regard to dreams, and so he immediately concluded that this was a symbolic reflection of Jung's struggle with his latent homosexuality. He proclaimed his discovery to Jung with a sense of triumph. 'But,' declared Jung after being told so bluntly what his problem was, 'the eggs were scrambled!' We need to acknowledge that there is always a danger of imposing an interpretation upon a dream. A useful rule of thumb is to say that the interpretation that seems right to the dreamer and coheres with his feelings when awake (as well as within the dream) is usually the right one. It is for this reason that I have developed a reflective listening approach to dream inter-pretation, which respects the dreamer's material and works within their own ability to make connections between their dream and their waking life. Most of our dreams are to do with our ordinary day-to-day lives but they occasionally plumb the depths of our fears and personal struggles, and then they take the form of nightmares. It is important that we find ways of reliably opening our dream and working through it without distorting its message. For me, the essential clue to the real meaning is not through the window of the symbols it may contain but by paying careful attention to the feelings 'within' the dream. By comparing those 'inner' feelings with events in waking life that carry the same feel-ings, we are in effect building a bridge between the dream and the waking life event on which it is a comment.

The episode in Daniel that we have just read is a unique example of dream work in the Bible, in that it is the therapist or helper who describes the dream to the dreamer and not the other way around! For Nebuchadnezzar, this dream hit him so hard that he could not go back to sleep and forget it. So let us look at the feelings within Nebuchadnezzar's dream and try to understand why he was so agitated.

The story behind the dream

This first recorded dream of the newly crowned King Nebuchadnezzar was to do with his role as kingdom leader and sustainer, and he was profoundly upset by the feelings it left him with. Somehow the dream threatened his perception of himself as the reigning monarch of the newest superpower in the Middle East. As king of Babylon from 605 to 562 BC, he was renowned as the most distinguished ruler of the Ne-Babylonian (Chaldean) dynasty founded by his father Nabopolassar. He was also the conqueror of Jerusalem who destroyed the city, deported the bulk of its inhabitants and assassinated every member of its royal house except Zedekiah, whom he ritually blinded before dragging him off to exile.

Nebuchadnezzar was an extremely competent general in his father's army and he successfully defeated the Egyptians at the battle of Carchemish in 606 BC, thereby opening up Syria and Palestine to his domination. He is also acclaimed as the rebuilder of Babylon, its walls, palaces, temples and defences, along with the famous 'Hanging Gardens' which were acknowledged as a wonder of the ancient world. He received tribute from a host of minor kingdoms and his power appeared to be supreme. There was no evidence of palace intrigues or rival kingdoms to threaten his hold on power. Yet he was so disturbed by this dream, early on in his reign, that perhaps inwardly he was already wrestling with feelings of insecurity and pride over his achievements. He needed to understand why he felt the panic he did, and it is for this reason that he was not simply going to let his court astrologers and magicians pacify him with interpretations that seemed right to them but not to him.

When Nebuchadnezzar summons his wise men and astrologers, he asks for the impossible: he not only wants an interpretation to his dream, he wants them actually to be able to tell him his dream

(Daniel 2:5–12). He tells them, 'I had a dream that I can't get out of my mind. I can't sleep until I know what it means' (2:3, *The Message*). He is every inch the despot who can treat the lives of others cheaply while at the same time exalting his own well-being to a level far above anyone or anything in his kingdom. So he resolutely informs them, 'This is what I have firmly decided: If you do not tell me what my dream was and interpret it, I will have you cut into pieces and your houses turned into piles of rubble' (2:5, NIV). The astrologers protest, saying that no king, no matter how powerful, has ever made such an impossible demand of his wise men.

We need to remind ourselves that the king is not asking the astrologers to tell him the dream because he has forgotten it but for precisely the opposite reason. Nebuchadnezzar knows very well what he has dreamed but he needs a deep reassurance that he is being understood and not being played around with.

The astrologers badly upset the king by saying that only God can answer such a demand and that the gods do not live among mortals (2:10–11). Most despots of that day (and since) assumed that they were semi-divine themselves or, at the very least, favoured by the gods. The astrologers had just made the fatal mistake of reducing Nebuchadnezzar to the status of a mere mortal, and he was enraged by both their impotence and their audacity. In his fury he orders the immediate execution of all the wise men in his government, and it is this command that catches Daniel and his three friends in the crossfire of the king's anger (2:12–13).

The opening two chapters of the book of Daniel present us with an interesting contrast between the mightiest man in the land and one of the newest arrivals, who was not much more than an educated slave. As we have seen, Nebuchadnezzar is so self-centred that he does not care about anything but his own needs, while Daniel's first action is to try to save not only himself but also his three fellow Hebrew slaves, as well as the entire court of astrologers (2:16). Daniel, Hananiah, Mishael and Azariah were probably some of the young children connected with the royal family who escaped the massacres when Jerusalem was destroyed (1:3). They were schooled and cultured in Babylonian ways, and even had their names changed to make them acceptable to court society: they were now to call themselves by the names of Belteshazzar, Shadrach, Meshach and Abednego (1:4–7). This was a clear attempt to remove their identity and completely immerse them in a Babylonian spirituality and lifestyle. Young as they were, however, they refused to forget the faith of their homeland and asked to be excused the dietary laws of their master's house. God blessed and sustained them in their stand for him: their health did not deteriorate and the blessing of God was so plainly upon them that they gained the respect of their captors (1:8–16). Because of their obedience to the Lord, we are told that they were granted wisdom and learning and that Daniel especially had the gift to understand visions and dreams (1:17). This gift was greatly used in his life and would, in the not-so-distant future, save his own life and those of his friends. Indeed, the ability to interpret dreams proves to be Daniel's core ministry to all the monarchs he serves and forms the cornerstone of the entire book named after him.

When Daniel learns of the king's outburst and the horror of its implications, he quickly asks to see the king, who had met him before and showed appreciation of his skill (1:19–20). Daniel manages to persuade Nebuchadnezzar to agree to a stay of execution while he prepares himself to interpret the dream (2:14–16). Daniel and his friends pray to God for his help and mercy, because they know that only he can understand dreams and interpret them. The answer comes in a dream vision when Daniel is asleep. This is the only occasion in the whole of scripture when we are told that a dream is given which interprets or explains another dream. Before going in to see the king, Daniel is keen to give credit where credit is due: he praises and exalts God, the one who reveals what is hidden in darkness, for his power and mercy (2:20–23). Interestingly enough, Daniel tells the king just what the astrologers had said, namely that only God can know and interpret this dream (2:27). The difference is, however, that Daniel believes in a God who communicates with those who love and worship him. The contrast between the statements of Daniel and the astrologers is apparently lost on the king, but he is about to find out why the dream disturbed him so much.

Learning the dream message

Daniel tells the king that in his dream vision he has seen a colossal human statue of brilliant and terrifying aspect. It is, in fact, a multi-metalled man. The description begins with the golden head—this was the usual title given to the monarchs of the oriental world kingdoms, and so Nebuchadnezzar would have understood that this part of the statue was a picture of his own kingdom (2:36–38). In fact, the statue represents the four successive kingdoms of Babylon, Media, Persia and Greece—the last three being taken up in more detail throughout the prophecies of Daniel. The dream is a sweeping prophetic insight into the future. The subsequent kingdoms are described as inferior to that of Nebuchadnezzar, but in reality they were greater in extent and power than Babylon. Judging from the increasing sense of disintegration and disunity of the metals as the giant statue is described, the 'inferiority' of the later kingdoms could be a reference to the fact that, no matter how strong in military might those kingdoms might be, they would have the fatal flaws of an increasingly degenerate morality, which would prove their downfall.

Nebuchadnezzar would have been very distressed to hear that his own kingdom was not going to be permanent but would be conquered by successive foreign kings. His own name meant '[the god] Nabu has protected the succession', and so his actual identity was under siege in this dream. Judging by his reactions when he awoke, he had had some intuitive feeling that this was the dream's message.

The fact that all four powers are insecure is convincingly demonstrated by the sudden impact of a rock, cut out of the mountain by supernatural means, which destroys the whole connection of kingdoms as it smashes into the feet of the statue and brings the colossus crashing to the ground. So forceful is the impact that the whole statue is reduced to dust and rubble and is lost without trace. 'It was like scraps of old newspapers in a vacant lot in a hot dry summer, blown every which way by the wind, scattered to oblivion' (2:35, *The Message*). The dream is saying that no matter how powerful a kingdom may be, God's power can remove it in an instant and prepare the way for the kingdom of heaven, which will rule for ever. The rock would become a mountain which would eclipse all the kingdoms that preceded it.

Buried inside the terrifying vision is a very important statement, which the king either refused or was unable to acknowledge—as we shall see from how he responded to the dream. Daniel informs Nebuchadnezzar that his power to rule is a gift from God. 'The God of heaven has given you dominion and power and might and glory; in your hands he has placed mankind and the beasts of the field and the birds of the air . . . You are that head of gold' (2:37–38, NIV). This recognition is a call to godly stewardship and care of people and of the creation itself. It has a curiously modern ring to it and, as Christians, we need to say loud and clear, to a world more conscientiously committed than we are to saving the environment, that part of the good news is that we are called to care for the earth and everyone in it. A great many New Age concerns should be ours too! Yet does the king realize that the main message of the prophecy is that he should recognize the true source of his power? We shall see.

Following the dream

Nebuchadnezzar responds in two basic ways to the interpretation of the terrifying dream that prevented him from sleeping: he is relieved, and he rebels against it. Due to the enormity of his relief, he immediately acknowledges the rightness of the interpretation and Daniel's obvious wisdom and gifting from his god. He prostrates himself and makes offerings and gives gifts to Daniel (2:46–48). Nebuchadnezzar also praises Yahweh as the chief among the gods, but not as God alone. He merely gives Yahweh a place of honour in his pantheon of gods as a good dream interpreter. The king also promotes Daniel and his three friends to places of prominence in his government of Babylon (2:49). There is an obvious parallel with the story of Joseph, who was also promoted to high office in the land that had formerly held him captive, and this reflects the serious respect given to those who were wise about the way of dreams.

So far, so good, we may say, but unfortunately it was not to last. No matter how much the king acknowledges Yahweh, he does not take to heart the core truth of the dream that his power comes from above and not from his own might. This, it seems, he could not accept. We can only guess what Nebuchadnezzar intended to do about the rest of the dream: judging by subsequent events, it seems that he tried to wipe its unpleasant message from his mind and do something to establish his rule more powerfully still.

Nebuchadnezzar, perhaps remembering the upsetting vision of the colossal multi-metalled statue, goes one better and builds a giant statue made entirely from gold (Daniel 3). We are not told in whose image the statue was made, but judging by the fact that it was of gold and that this was a symbol of the monarch's power to live and rule for ever, it would in all likelihood have been of the king himself. Everyone is commanded to bow down and worship, and there are to be no exceptions. However, Shadrach, Meshach and Abednego refuse to give up their love for God by idolizing the king's golden image. They are thrown into a fiery furnace to burn to death, in order to satisfy the insatiable appetite of the despot for total power and the complete subservience of his people. Despite previously acknowledging Yahweh, the king has returned to his old habits. However, the three friends having been thrown into the blazing furnace, one 'like a son of the gods' walks among them dazzlingly, and they are delivered without even a smell of smoke upon their bodies (3:25–27). Once more the king acknowledges the God of heaven, changes his plans and is merciful. But as we shall see, he was not so easily turned from his desire to parade his power and might.

Making it personal

Why did the king rebel so bluntly against a dream that he had formerly accepted as a true word from God? Perhaps the answer is quite simple and reflects our own habits also: he simply did not want to change. He could not afford the price of opening up to God to guide and lead his life; his pride would not let him. Being the despot that he was, he did not choose to ignore his dream—he flagrantly rebelled against it and built the statue of gold. This is a picture of a person already falling apart because he is fighting against what he actually believes. It is inevitable, therefore, that he will ultimately destroy himself. Anyone who has had a minimum of experience as a qualified counsellor will recognize the symptoms as already present in King Nebuchad-nezzar. The king's dilemma, in fact, highlights a truth about dreams acknowledged by most of the pioneers in this field of work—that we are more honest when we are asleep than when we are awake. There are a number of reasons to explain this. We give ourselves little time in waking life to be aware of what is going on within us and around us, because of the pressures and pace of life that many of us face. There is also the issue of peer group pressure and the many voices that want to tell us the opposite of what we really think. It takes a brave person to go against this kind of flow in life. Another reason is the fears that we often have about what will happen to us, or what people will think of us, if we do something that sets us apart from what others have come to expect of us. When we go to sleep, however, these restraints are often far less powerful or completely absent from our dreams. To put it another way, we will tell ourselves things when we are asleep that we would not dream of telling ourselves when we are awake!

Therefore, we should not invest our dreams with more than they actually contain, but we should none the less respect them and pay attention to what they are saying. When appropriate, we should perhaps share our dreams with someone we trust, and pray about how we want to follow through the messages or statements we have been making when asleep. According to Herman Riffel, our dreams are an invaluable source of spiritual insight:

> The dream is an invaluable counsellor. We cannot pray for a better one. It is with us every night, charges no fees, and makes no demands except that we listen to it and learn to detect God's voice in symbolic language. The dream seeks to co-operate with his great purpose; to help us to realize every part of our potential and to bring us into harmony with ourselves, God and the world around us. There is no better way to get to the heart of our problems than through our dreams.[1]

Prayer

Lord God of all my pathways,
help me to take the good way,
the right way,
the only way.

Lord God of every decision I make,
show me the best choice,
the true choice,
the authentic choice.

Lord God of all my moments,
hold my good times,
forgive my sinful times,
celebrate my best times,
and see you in my end time.
Amen

10

Seeing the Lord of all things

Nebuchadnezzar's testimony to healing and wholeness

——◆◆◆——

I . . . raised my eyes toward heaven, and my sanity was restored. Then I praised the Most High; I honoured and glorified him who lives for ever.   *Daniel 4:34 (NIV)*

The dream

This is the vision which came to me while I lay on my bed: As I was looking, there appeared a very lofty tree at the centre of the earth; the tree grew great and became strong; its top reached the sky, and it was visible to the earth's farthest bounds. Its foliage was beautiful and its fruit abundant, and it yielded fruit for all. Beneath it the wild beasts found shelter, the birds lodged in its branches, and from it all living creatures fed.

This is what I saw in the vision which came to me while I lay on my bed: There appeared a watcher, a holy one coming down from heaven. In a mighty voice he cried, 'Hew down the tree, lop off the branches, strip away its foliage and scatter the fruit; let the wild beasts flee from beneath it and the birds from its branches; but leave the stump with its roots in the ground. So, bound with iron and bronze among the lush grass, let him be drenched with the dew of heaven and share the lot of the beasts in their pasture—his mind will cease to be human, and he will be given the mind of a beast. Seven times will pass over him. The issue has been determined by the watchers and the sentence pronounced by the holy ones. Thereby the living will

know that the Most High is sovereign in the kingdom of men:
he gives the kingdom to whom he wills, and may appoint
over it the lowliest of mankind.'   *Daniel 4:10–17 (REB)*

What is remarkable about this dream is that it is given as part of
the testimony of a king who had finally learned the lesson of his
lifetime—that Yahweh is the one who is really Lord of all things,
including the power of earthly kingdoms, no matter how extensive.
Some commentators have suggested that this whole chapter was
written at a later date by the king's enemies in order to discredit
him and his empire. The one outstanding characteristic of this
testimony, however, is the dignity and the depth with which Yahweh
is recognized and worshipped as the ever living and supreme Lord.
I have always found that when people authentically give praise to
God, they are themselves given respect and honour by the process.
Because the king's dream forms part of his testimony, we know
immediately that it is part of the learning curve that the testimony
is aimed at demonstrating. Before we unpack the dream, therefore,
we are alerted to the fact that it is going to teach us something
about what the dreamer has learned about himself and about God.

From his opening remarks, we see a different spirit in the king.
He is no longer issuing orders and demands but saying that it
gives him pleasure to speak of the miraculous signs that God had
revealed to him (4:2–3). He addresses God as the 'most high God',
which is one of the ancient Semitic terms for deity and which
enjoyed something of a revival in use at about this time. Most
interestingly of all, the king begins his testimony by describing his
own empire as part of God's kingdom which is an eternal kingdom
(4:3). From his opening address alone, we realize that something
profound has happened to him to change him in this way, and
we are about to be told what it is.

It is worth noting that the dream has two main parts, con-
veying quite different approaches to the dream story. In the first
part, the dreamer is essentially a spectator watching a picture unfold
(4:10–12); in the second segment of the dream, the dreamer is a
participant in the action and is challenged directly by an angel

(4:13–17). When we move from observer to actor in a dream, this reveals that it is about an event with which we have been involved and which we now feel is coming to some kind of climax or conclusion. The dream acts as a rehearsal for the waking event which we feel is shortly going to happen.

Both parts of the dream are described as 'visions': Nebuchadnezzar is saying that they had a prophetic element, a word from God about a situation that concerned or involved Nebuchadnezzar as the dreamer (4:10, 13). Prophecy does include revealing future events that God is planning, but to a greater degree it is about receiving God's perspective on a matter which is usually already known to us. And of course, God's viewpoint may be radically different from our own!

In Nebuchadnezzar's case, it seems that in the beginning he had the attitude to power typical of a despot. He was convinced that power was his by right of his own strength and achievements, and that he could do as he liked with his power, without fear of recriminations from his critics or enemies. He showed no apparent sign of contrition or remorse about his threats to destroy the entire company of court astrologers if they failed to satisfy his need to understand his first dream. Although he showed wonder at the survival of Daniel's three friends in the fiery furnace, and caught glimpses of the divine 'son of man' among them, he did not apologize to them or repent of his actions. Instead, he threatened to cut to pieces anyone who spoke evil of the God of Shadrach, Meshach and Abednego! (Daniel 3:29). He was still exercising his power to kill and destroy almost at a whim, even if his whim concerned the living God.

As we shall see, the whole point of the king's testimony now is to say that he has learned the lesson of how God saw him and he has been changed for the better.

The story behind the dream

It is important to get the timing of this dream into perspective. Nebuchadnezzar tells us that it was the year after having the dream that things went drastically wrong in his life (4:29–32). He points out that he was walking on the roof of the royal palace at the time, and as the palace was completed later in his reign it seems reasonable to say that this dream occurred in the second half of his 43 years as king. The dream of the multi-metalled man took place in the second year of his reign (2:1), so a period of 25 to 30 years had passed by since then. You can forget a lot in that number of years if you want to! Dulled from his memory was the disturbing dream that had required the immediate attention of his best astrologers; gone from his thoughts was the dazzling spectacle of three men coming unsinged from a furnace. The king had submerged himself in his power and prosperity and, on the surface of things, he looked contented and prosperous (4:4). Interestingly enough, the Hebrew word for 'prosper' means 'the growing green of the fresh vigorous growth of a tree' (compare Psalms 52:8; 92:12) and is an obvious play on the dream picture.

Nebuchadnezzar had already been challenged about recognizing that God was the real power behind his throne, but he had turned his back on those words. Donald J. Wiseman says that if Nebuchadnezzar struggled with anything during the last years of his rule, it was more than likely the seeds of economic decline resulting from the cost of his enterprises.[1] If this is so, the king may well have been concerned about the demands to maintain his empire, but as yet he was not losing much sleep over it. Yet God remembers when we forget, and we must not mistake years of silence as years of neglect. They offer us a chance to receive his mercy and change our ways. The king had done neither, however, and this was why he was so terrified when, in a dream, God renewed the challenge to his life and monarchy.

Learning the dream message

The king dreamed of another colossus, only this time it was a tree. It was a giant tree and still growing tall although its leaves were touching heaven. The picture is almost a re-creation of the garden of Eden. The tree gives life to all that feed off it and find shelter in its branches. The fruit is very pleasing to the eye and super-abundant. This is a mythical tree but one that represents a world rule whose power stretches over the whole earth. I am sure that Nebuchadnezzar would have had no difficulty in making this connection for himself. It is not this that makes the dream terrifying, it is what comes next as the king is more and more drawn into the dream himself.

A watchman or angel comes out of heaven and, without wasting any time, orders the destruction of the tree. Apart from its trunk, it is to be utterly destroyed, rather like the colossal statue of the earlier dream. Nebuchadnezzar doesn't say it, but you can feel the panic that he must have felt in his bones. Then, suddenly, the angel turns and speaks to the terrified king: he will be reduced to living like an animal, out of his mind, without an empire and with no companionship except for the beasts of the field (4:15–16). The angel grimly informs him that he will live in this state for 'seven times', which may be a reference to a literal seven years, although this is unlikely as the king would hardly have returned to power if he had been mentally sick for such a long time. The term may in fact indicate an unspecified but not too lengthy period of time.

There is no mention of what will happen next, as the dream ends abruptly with a statement from the angel, to the effect that God is sovereign over every empire and he can give its leadership to whom he pleases, even the weakest or most lowborn of people (4:17).

No wonder the king wakes up in alarm! The dream threatens to topple him from power and reduce him to insanity. He wants help or reassurance, and once again he is determined to get it. This time, he is going to be warned even when he is awake. But will he heed the lesson? We shall see.

Following the dream

Once again the king is panicked into summoning his astrologers immediately to his court to help him understand his dream message. This time there are no games, just a frank sharing of the dream, but the wise men are unable to interpret it (4:6–7). Perhaps they were unwilling to do so, because of the message it contained. It seems that Daniel is an afterthought in the king's mind and is summoned last of all. As Daniel had been so successful before, you would have thought that Nebuchadnezzar would have asked him to come first, Although we are not specifically told, it seems that the king is hoping that his own people will give a favourable interpretation, one that will explain away the terror and make his world all right once again. He may well have remembered, despite the passing of almost 30 years, that Daniel would tell him the truth—a truth that he was unwilling or afraid to face—and so he put off summoning Daniel until he had no choice.

The beginnings of humility can be seen in the way the king recognizes that Daniel has the spirit of the gods in him (4:9, 18) and that dream work is his gift. This is not an acknowledgment of the one God, Yahweh, but a recognition that Daniel is specially gifted. And so he shares his dream fully with Daniel, whose initial response is to be very perplexed about what to tell the king: the news is not good. It is at this point that the king accepts that the dream was about his own downfall. He wants to hear the truth and so encourages Daniel to get on with sharing what he knows (4:19).

The process of the dream interpretation is interesting to follow. Daniel reflects back to the king a summary of the dream, largely using the words that Nebuchadnezzar had used to describe his dream. Daniel does not just tell him the meaning: there is a real concern to engage the king in his own dream interpretation work. The practice of reflecting back what the speaker has said is one of the recognized elements in active listening skills. It conveys to the speaker that they have really been heard, empowers them to own their material at a greater depth within themselves and also serves to clarify the mixture of feelings and thoughts with which they may have been struggling.

The king is now properly prepared for the hardest part of the interpretation, namely that the destroyed tree is the king himself (4:20–25). Nebuchadnezzar is told that the Most High God has issued a decree to drive him out of his kingdom and into the bizarre life of a madman living among cattle and looking a terrible mess. This condition is to continue until Nebuchadnezzar acknowledges the challenge that had come in his dream nearly 30 years earlier, namely that the Most High is sovereign over his kingdom (4:25). Daniel offers some hope in this darkness: the image of leaving the tree trunk intact but bound with bronze and iron is a promise that Nebuchadnezzar's kingdom will be restored to him when he accepts the dream message that the Most High reigns. Daniel ends his dream interpretation by challenging the king, as boldly as he dare, to repent and change his ways and become more caring for the poor and oppressed in his kingdom (4:27). It is not often that people have the courage to speak out to a despot in such a direct and confrontative way: they usually die for the privilege! It is possible that Daniel saw into the king's heart, realized that the dream had really penetrated his mind, and he decided that it was 'now or never'. Would the king listen this time?

The king did absolutely nothing! He did not have Daniel put to death for speaking so directly to him, nor is there an account of promoting Daniel or honouring him for his wisdom. There is no record of anything at all except the king simply carrying on as before. Daniel's plea to repent had fallen on deaf ears and a hard heart, it seemed. However, in his testimony Nebuchadnezzar describes the dramatic turning point in his life, when his dream message came back to haunt him. A year later he was walking the rooftop verandas of his newly built royal palace, wallowing in a moment of sheer self-indulgence as he praised himself for his own glory and majesty (4:30). Was this the first evidence of megalomania, which is often a feature in the lives of those who wield absolute power? If so, the king was showing signs of the mental fragmentation about which he had been warned before. Suddenly the judgment of God was upon the king and he did indeed lose his mind and end up eating grass like the cattle he owned (4:31–33).

Healing came only when the king took to heart his dream message from God. He testifies, 'I raised my eyes toward heaven, and my sanity was restored. Then I praised the Most High; I honoured and glorified him who lives for ever' (4:34, NIV). Somewhere in his tortured life he remembered the ways in which God had spoken to him and he finally got the message; his look to the God of heaven was an unwritten song of repentance and a cry for help.

Nebuchadnezzar is transformed from the king who struts his way through life full of pomp and pride, to become the monarch who gladly shares where his power truly lies, in the God of heaven. He pours out his song of praises to God and recognizes that God's kingdom rules for ever. The whole climax of this testimony is summed up in his closing description of how he now lives his life: 'Now I, Nebuchadnezzar, praise and exalt and glorify the King of heaven, because everything he does is right and all his ways are just. And those who walk in pride he is able to humble' (4:37, NIV). These are the words of a man who has experienced what he is talking about. This is no empty singing of a shallow song. It is the worship of a man who has suffered to gain faith and insight into God's ways and who has learned to die to his pride and live in the life that God supplies. It is costly praise, and there is no other kind to offer God.

Making it personal

One of the most attractive things about God is his capacity to forgive us and set us back on the pathway to newness of life. God worked in Nebuchadnezzar's heart for over 30 years. He did not give up when the king rebelled, or threatened to kill, or simply tried to forget that God had spoken to him. Our faithful and cherishing God persevered down the years and, even when he confronted the king so dramatically, it was not to condemn him and leave him in the darkness of his own madness but to turn him towards the light of eternity. It is amazing but true that the Lord is always taking the rubbish we create and redeeming it through his work at Calvary. This does not in any way make right the wrong things we have done, but it does illustrate that we have a God who can turn wrongs to our good and to his glory. Nebuchadnezzar learnt how to be a worshipper of the living God from the schoolroom of insanity; the apostle Paul learnt how to love and teach the word of God from a background of religious pride; and John learnt to see the dazzling radiance of the King of kings in the prison regime he endured on the island of Patmos.

I remember some years ago, when I had made a mess of many things in my life, going to a healing service at a conference in Canterbury. When the invitation came to receive prayer with the laying on of hands, I made sure I was prayed with by someone who knew nothing of my problems. After a moment of silence as she laid her hands upon my head, she spoke these words over me: 'I see a picture of an oak tree which has been badly hit in a storm. It has been reduced to almost a stump and half of its roots have been lost. Yet there are still enough roots left for the tree to grow again and regain its full stature.' I was touched that God would speak to me in this way as I was feeling very lonely and was struggling with my faith. It helped me to turn away from despair and look again to the God who loved me and had made me his son—to dare to believe that his love would go on and on for me. As someone once said who had spent years living for their Lord, 'There is nothing you can do to make God love you more; and there is nothing you can do, no sin, which will make him love you any less.' This is not to make us complacent about our need to repent sometimes and straighten out our lives, but it does give us the energy to dare to run into the arms of a heavenly Father who is waiting to give us that love.

Prayer

God of the second chance,
the last chance,
the only chance,
don't let go of me.
Give me another chance.

Son of the shepherd heart,
the broken heart,
the bursting heart,
don't let go of me.
Give me new heart.

Spirit of the eagle-eyed vision,
the heavenly vision,
the nightmare vision,
don't let go of me.
Give me renewed vision.

Amen

11

A *model father*

Joseph's marriage dream

'You are to give him the name Jesus, because he will save his people from their sins.' *Matthew 1:21 (NIV)*

The dream

An angel of the Lord appeared to him in a dream and said, 'Joseph son of David, do not be afraid to take Mary home as your wife, because what is conceived in her is from the Holy Spirit. She will give birth to a son, and you are to give him the name Jesus, because he will save his people from their sins.' *Matthew 1:20–21 (NIV)*

What is remarkable about this dream is that there is no visual content described, only the monologue of the angel of the Lord. There are no powerful or blazing lights, no collapsing on the ground by the one beholding the angel as their strength vanishes at this marvellous sight. The dream is presented in a rather matter-of-fact fashion: it consists of a short speech from heaven and comes with all the authority of a divine command. We are all familiar with the Christmas story and how it abounds with angelic appearances and warnings. Most of these angelic encounters take place within dreams, but unfortunately we usually leave our appreciation of angels and dreams there—as a Christmas event only, and of no further use to us. However, there are numerous incidents involving angels in the Bible and over 100 references to dreams and visions; they are both major subjects and should be given due respect. Herman Riffel has gone so far as to say that if we added together all the direct references to dreams and visions, all the stories surrounding them and all the prophecies that issued out of them, this material would cover about one-third of the entire Bible.[1]

Angels are God's messengers, delivering the word and warnings of God to his servants. According to scripture, they were sent to assist Jesus as he recovered from the onslaught of direct temptation from Satan (Matthew 4:11) and as he prayed in the garden of Gethsemane, battling with his determination to be obedient to death on a cross (Luke 22:43). Angels rescued some of the apostles from prison by appearing in the middle of the night and encouraging them to go free and preach the gospel in the temple courts (Acts 5:19–20). When the angel of the Lord burst into Peter's lonely prison cell to do the same for him, Peter had to be almost manhandled to freedom, because he thought that it was only a vision he was having in his sleep! (Acts 12:7–9). It was an angel who commanded Philip to go and loiter with intent on a desert highway in the Gaza strip, where he was able to witness to the Ethiopian eunuch and send him back to his home country rejoicing in God (Acts 8:26–39).

Angels also come to announce news from God, and it is for this reason that the angel named Gabriel appeared to Mary to tell her that she was going to give birth to God's son (Luke 1:26–37). The angel Gabriel also informed the ageing Zechariah that, after years of prayer, God was about to answer his deepest longing and empower his wife to conceive and bear a son who would become known as John the Baptist (Luke 1:5–17). In both cases, the angel's first words of greeting were 'Do not be afraid.' Presumably this was because of the startling or outstanding appearance of the angel: when Zechariah saw the angel he was 'startled and gripped with fear' (Luke 1:12). Many years previously, Daniel had encountered Gabriel, and he was terrified and fell on his face on the ground (Daniel 8:15–17).

The 'angel of the Lord' is a common term in the Bible, and it is usually assumed to be an indication that God speaks through whatever agencies (such as angels) he might choose—because the only direct speech he had with any person was when he spoke with Moses face to face (Numbers 12:8). The angel of the Lord appears to Hagar and her baby son Ishmael, who are trying to survive on their own in the desert, and encourages them that they will one day be founders of a nation (Genesis 16:7–13). It is the angel of the Lord who prevents Abraham from sacrificing his teenage son Isaac in his ultimate act of trust in God (Genesis 22:11–12). It is the angel of the Lord who appears to Moses in the flames of the burning bush (Exodus 3:2). Some commentators have suggested that these Old Testament accounts are references to the pre-existent Christ appearing in visible form; we have no real evidence for this, although it is not beyond the bounds of possibility. Let us at least positively accept and be open to the ministry of angels to us, as was Joseph. After all, we need all the help we can get from God!

Joseph's first dream consists of a simple but commanding speech. The fact that it is delivered by an angel of the Lord does not seem to deter or upset him. I think that this is not only because he was a man whose faith must have been deep and mature but because the words in his dream exactly matched the personal turmoil he was going through. It came as a relief to have some direction in his life. Let us try to get to know something of this man and understand why he was ready to listen to the angel when it came to him in his sleep.

The story behind the dream

We know very little about Joseph. Except in the stories about Jesus' infancy, he is totally absent from the Gospel narratives, and most people have concluded from this that he must have died by the time Jesus was an adult. However, he is probably the most important figure, apart from Mary, in Jesus' early life, helping to shape him towards his manhood and giving him insights into the character of God.

Joseph is introduced to us by Matthew as the son of Jacob, and a direct descendant of King David (Matthew 1:16). The only other biographical detail we are given is that he was betrothed to Mary and that the engagement had not been consummated into formal marriage. There was commonly an interval of ten to twelve months between engagement and the celebration of the nuptials (compare Deuteronomy 20:7; 24:5; Judges 14:8). It was during this period of partial separation that Joseph discovered that his betrothed was pregnant, and the one thing he knew was that he was not the father of the child. We can only guess at how heartbroken and depressed he must have felt, because there was no question that the nuptial celebrations would have to be cancelled and the whole marriage contract dissolved through divorce. He concluded along with everybody else that Mary had had an affair with another man: he had been betrayed.

Despite the pain of disillusionment and the destruction of his dreams, however, the character of Joseph radiates out from the pages of the Bible. He would have been perfectly within his rights to divorce Mary according to all the expected procedures and, in so doing, to affirm and underline his own innocence and hurt. Divorce would have entailed a public meeting with witnesses who would countersign the divorce document, and the reasons for the action would have been read out for all to hear (Deuteronomy 24:1). Also, unfaithfulness during this period of betrothal was regarded as adultery (Deuteronomy 22:25, 28), and the punishment was severe. In countries like Egypt it involved cutting off the nose, and in Persia at that time it also involved cutting off the ears. Judaic law required the death penalty (Deuteronomy 22:23–24) and, as in the case of the woman hauled before Jesus for punishment, it was normally carried out by stoning (John 8:5). This was the horrific prospect for Mary as Joseph tried to come to terms with the news of her pregnancy and decide what he would do.

It is now that his greatness of character shines out above law and beyond principles, and reflects God's father-heart of goodness and love. As much as he was in the right to demand justice publicly, he is none the less thinking of Mary's welfare more than his own dearly held principles. His focus is on her need, even though he is the wronged person. This is so much like Christ who, though we have sinned against him, wants to go on finding ways to offer us freedom and healing. Joseph is described as a 'just man' (1:19) and, judging by the context, this is not a statement of the right standing that his friends thought he held before God but rather a description of the fact that he was a good and merciful man. This is reflected in the fact that he wants to end the relationship without getting public vindication, so that Mary can have space to adjust and get on with her life without public shame. The word used here in verse 19 for 'secretly' or 'privately' is the Greek word *lathra*, which literally means 'to escape notice'. Joseph was certainly hurting, but he loved Mary so much that he wanted to minimize the damage to her so that she could have a future in the community.

As we read this story, perhaps our minds are already racing ahead to Mary's destiny and the birth of her son Jesus, and Joseph is already receding into the background of our thoughts. But stop a minute and ask yourself what the consequences would be for Joseph because of his magnanimous heart? He was willing to embrace a future without the woman he loved and perhaps to live alone for the rest of his life. He was probably much older than Mary, so this is not so far-fetched an idea. There is no evidence that he had already been married and had other children to comfort him in his old age. This was a man who was willing to embrace emotional oblivion to help the person who had hurt him the most. In this he prefigures the sacrifice of Jesus, who embraced the sins of the world and stepped into the darkness of the cross of death in order that we, whom he loves most, might be saved. It was these thoughts of loss and future loneliness that Joseph was wrestling with as he went to sleep on that fateful evening.

Learning the dream message

Everything changes radically overnight. The angel of the Lord appears, but there is no description of his appearance or of what Joseph thinks about it. The appearance of the angel pales into insignificance compared with the message that is given. It is utterly astounding, to say the least. The father of the baby is the Holy Spirit of the living God, and the boy child to be born will be the saviour of a nation (Matthew 1:20–21).

To be addressed by the angel as 'son of David' would immediately have struck a messianic chord in Joseph's memory, as this was one of the official descriptions of the Messiah. Ideas of the gods having sexual relationships with mortals were common to other religions of the time, such as within the Greek pantheon, with Zeus impregnating the mother of Heracles.[2] This was unheard of within the Judaic tradition, however, and at first would have been offensive to Joseph's ears. The very idea of God also being human was considered blasphemous, as is witnessed by the attempts of the Pharisees to stone Jesus when he claimed to be divine by taking for himself the very name of God: 'Before Abraham was, I am' (John 8:58–59).

The second half of the dream message is a prophecy that the boy yet to be born will be the saviour of the world. The name Jesus would have been very common in Joseph's day, but it is the baby's calling rather than his name that carries most impact. So, on the one hand, Joseph is faced with the possibility of Mary having had illicit sex with a person unknown. On the other, he receives the astounding revelation that God has stepped into their lives to do a totally new and radical thing. Which is he to believe?

Following the dream

It seems that, without hesitation, Joseph responds by cementing his engagement and marrying Mary. There is no record of her response to his determination to marry her or his conviction that she is indeed pregnant through a divine and mysterious act of the Holy Spirit. He honours and respects her pregnancy by abstaining from sexual intercourse with her until Jesus is born. This is a colossal step of faith on his part. Who knows how his friends may have taunted him for his actions and called him a fool? Yet his love for Mary helps him to recognize her integrity—and no doubt Elizabeth, Mary's cousin, would have helped to explain her condition. So Joseph takes the irrevocable step of marrying Mary and leaving for Bethlehem in obedience to the Roman summons to return to his place of origin in order to be properly included in the census (Luke 2:1–7). Joseph is there to greet the arrival of the Magi from the East and shepherds from the valley below. He endures the death threats of King Herod and the life of a refugee in Egypt before returning to Galilee, and Nazareth in particular.

Interestingly, it is to Joseph that the angel of the Lord reappears with warning dreams that have the effect of saving the family from the threat of death (Matthew 2:13, 19). It seems that he knows how to keep his dreams open to the entrance of angels bringing the word of the Lord, and he has the wisdom to act upon those dreams.

Joseph goes through the agonies of apparently losing Jesus before discovering him engaged in theological debate in the temple (Luke 2:41–50). Then Joseph simply disappears from the story as it jumps from the early teens of Jesus' life to his emergence as a young rabbi. Even then, the stigma of Jesus' parentage has not gone away, as is demonstrated by the cynical comments of those in Nazareth who describe Jesus as the 'son of Mary' (Mark 6:3). No Jewish boy was named after his mother and so this was a way of saying that one thing was certain: Joseph was not Jesus' father! Yet the mark of Joseph was deeply ingrained into the heart of Jesus and played a prominent role in his public teaching.

Humanly speaking, Jesus had no other model of fatherhood than Joseph. Donald Coggan, in his book *The Servant Son*, suggests that one of the reasons why Jesus spoke so much about the father-hood of God was that he saw a good example of what it meant to be a father in Joseph.[3] I think we can safely conclude that Joseph, though he died before Jesus reached full manhood, had provided an example as a father who had enriched and deepened Jesus' knowledge and awareness of the kind of father that God is. This kindly man who had saved his wife from shame also delivered to his son by marriage a picture of parenthood that built bridges of connection with God himself. Perhaps this is the greatest gift that Joseph can give to us and inspire us to—the desire and determination to live in such a way that we point people to the love of God, our heavenly Father.

Making it personal

Before he went to sleep, Joseph had made a decision about Mary. When he woke up the next day, he made a completely different choice. I don't think that this was just because the angel of the Lord visited him in his dream. It is quite plain that he was struggling with what to do and, in the end, had resolved to do the 'proper thing', but one wonders what his heart was saying. Surely he loved Mary, and was perhaps toying with ignoring the conventions of the day and going ahead with the marriage! The angel of the Lord stepped into his dream and helped him to see deeper into his heart and, in doing so, to learn some prophetic insights from God. I am reminded of that moment in C.S. Lewis' story The *Lion, the Witch and the Wardrobe* when Aslan comes shockingly and powerfully back to life after having been sacrificed on the stone altar. He is dazzling and bright and full of even more vigour and power than before his death. The children are stunned and, after the successful battle against their enemies, they ask him how it could have happened. Aslan says that the wicked witch only knew of one magic, but that he knew of an older and far more wise and powerful magic, the magic of the resurrection that would come into force when somebody gave up their life for another. It was seeing this deeper truth that sustained Aslan in his act of self-sacrifice.

Often our dreams challenge the perceptions we have in waking life. This is because we do not always listen closely enough to ourselves, to others or to God and therefore fail to pick up the warning signals that life presents. When we go to sleep, however, these denied messages surface and speak to us, challenging us to look afresh at the subject in hand. We are rather like a detective who sifts through the evidence and arrives at a surprising insight, but we do this while we are asleep. It is quite acceptable to think that God is involved in these times and that by his Spirit he is stirring us to listen and look again at the deeper truths we have ignored. And so, if you have a dream that offers you a different perspective on a situation, then pray about it and see if it does indeed spring from deeper depths, fitting the facts upon which you have been reflecting in sleep. Share it with a friend and, if it seems right, take appropriate action to follow it through.

Finally, cultivate the heart of a Joseph. He barely appears in Jesus' story, yet without him Jesus would not have known what it was to be fathered and so favoured. Without him, there would have been no holy family, only the tragedy of an unmarried mother—and a real danger that the baby would have perished in the vicious pogrom that Herod carried out against all the male children in Bethlehem. The Christmas story would have been a nightmare. Joseph is not on record for uttering noble sayings. There is no account that he did mighty exploits worthy of fame. He just quietly carried out the word that the Lord had showed him and poured his gentle love into his wife and children— so much so that one of his other sons, James, became a leader in the church in Jerusalem and showed his father's wise love in his openness to the radical departure of welcoming Gentiles into the Church of Jesus (Acts 15:13–19). Despite the voices of criticism around him, he remained steady and showed love and consideration to those whom the rules and conventions of his day would have cast out. I think that Joseph, though long gone from the scene, was still speaking through at least two of his sons. Let us, therefore, cultivate the loving gift of hoping for and working for the best in the wounded, and especially in those who have made a mess of their lives.

Prayer

Lord God of signs and wonders,
when sin has silenced our song
you celebrate the good you see in us.

Great Son, friend of all who stray,
when shame has broken our best
you plan for us a new and living way.

Wild Spirit with healing wings,
when lies destroy our standing
you warm us with a father's embracing.

Therefore,
we will run,
stagger with amazement,
and kneel in penitence,
because you
care for
us.
Amen

12

Saving Jesus

The Christmas warning dreams

God's angel showed up again . . . and commanded, 'Get up.
Take the child and his mother and flee to Egypt.'
Matthew 2:13 (The Message)

The dream

In a dream, [the Magi] were warned not to report back to
Herod . . . After the scholars were gone, God's angel showed
up again in Joseph's dream and commanded, 'Get up. Take the
child and his mother and flee to Egypt. Stay until further notice.
Herod is on the hunt for this child, and wants to kill him.' . . .
Later, when Herod died, God's angel appeared in a dream to
Joseph in Egypt: 'Up, take the child and his mother and return
to Israel. All those out to murder the child are dead . . .' Joseph
was directed in a dream to go to the hills of Galilee.
Matthew 2:12–13, 19–20, 22 (The Message)

Here are four warning dreams, all for the purpose of saving Jesus—
because this was one time in his life when he could not save
himself. There came another time when he could have called ten
thousand angels to deliver him from the cross, but he remained
silent (Matthew 26:53).

Three of these dreams are given to Joseph and one to the group
of Magi, or wise men, from the East. All of Joseph's messages are
delivered by an unnamed angel who appears in his dreams and
simply utters commands and directions. All the dreams carry a
sense of urgency about them because they are to be acted upon

immediately. Unlike many of our own dreams, these need no interpretation, only action. However, there will be times in our own lives when God may give us direct guidance through our dreams and, to a large degree, this conforms to the ways in which God can convict and challenge us in our waking lives. For example, think of the story of Dr T. J. Barnardo, who founded his work among orphaned children in London. He had trained and prepared to go to China to work with Hudson Taylor and the China Inland Mission. He was staying in London, waiting to catch the boat that would take him to the East, when he had a series of dreams compelling him to give up his decision to be a missionary and work with the abandoned children in the city. He had been wrestling with his conscience about which choice to make, and in his dream he felt that God told him to give up going abroad; the rest of the story is well known.[1]

Once again we must notice how the dream, even when it is from God, is usually connected with some event that we are confronting in waking life. We all have those 'nudges' in our experience, which make us think about things that perhaps we should do or that God may be calling us to do. But sometimes we are not sure, so we ignore or even forget about them. Sometimes the nudges persist for a while, but if we do not give them attention they often go away. Since we are more in touch with our denied agenda in sleep, however, we should not be surprised if God chooses this as the time and place to bring us his message of guidance. Consequently we should cultivate a prayerful response to this kind of dream message, and if it continues to come with authority then we should take a risk in faith and do what the message says. Of course we should first satisfy ourselves that it is a good, right and loving thing to do, and that it will please the Lord.

Morton Kelsey studied dreams for over ten years and came to the following conclusion about how they had affected his life:

> I discovered that my dreams were wiser than my well-tuned
> rational mind and that they gave me warnings when I was in

danger. They also described in symbols the disastrous situations in which I found myself. These strange messengers of the night offered suggestions on how to find my way out of lostness.

When I followed these symbolic suggestions, much of the darkness lifted, and my situation no longer seemed hopeless. Many of the psychological and physical symptoms of distress disappeared. In addition to all this, I found a very personal being at the heart of reality who cared for me . . . as I continued to listen to my dreams, I experienced the risen Christ in a way I had not thought possible.[2]

We are simply out of touch with our dreams and, if we are honest, if someone tells us that they believe God has spoken to them in their sleep we may be tempted to think that they are a little extreme. Yet the history of the kingdom of God is filled with examples of people hearing God in their sleep, stepping out in faith and obedience and achieving great things for the Lord. Saint Patrick in his *Confessions* tells of two dreams that changed his life. One alerted him to an opportunity to escape from his seven years of captivity in Ireland, and the other was a 'Macedonian call' to go back and evangelize Ireland.[3] John Bunyan gained his inspiration for *The Pilgrim's Progress* while he slept in an open shed as he went about preaching. John Newton's famous hymn 'Amazing Grace' was the result of a disturbing dream that helped to bring him to faith in Christ, and the founder of the Salvation Army, William Booth, once wrote that it was a dream of thousands perishing that determined him to devote his life to rescuing and restoring the lost.[4]

Hearing God speaking through dreams and visions was a normal experience for people in the days of Joseph and Mary. We have been the casualties of a gradual progression towards rationalism and scientific materialism, which has cast suspicion on the supernatural interventions of God into our life and society. Yet the wind of the Spirit is still blowing and there have been encouraging signs that we are waking up to the possibilities of hearing from God through dreams and visions.

The story behind the dream

Threading through all four warning dreams is the threat of murder. God was doing a spectacular thing—he was providing the universe with his saviour son! Heavenly light was breaking in on a dark world in which the voice of prophecy had been silent for over 200 years. Suddenly the skies were full of angels glorifying God, and dreams were invaded by heavenly beings intent on securing the well-being of a baby in whom would lie the salvation hope of all people. It was no less than the birth of the King of kings, and in the country of a despotic king well known for his capacity for cruelty.

The story opens with the arrival of the Magi. They come on camels from the East, which could mean Persia or Arabia. The word 'magi' has given us the word 'magicians'—who are usually given a negative press in the Bible—but in the book of Daniel the magicians are presented as court advisers who are unable to understand the dreams that God gives. In the New Testament there are the examples of Simon of Samaria, who manipulated people with his skills and was obsessed with power and control (Acts 8:9–24), and Bar-Jesus, who is described as a false prophet and who opposed the mission of Paul, to his own cost (Acts 13:6–12). Their interests ranged through astronomy, astrology, religion and medicine. This helps us to understand the Magi's fascination with following the star—which was probably a comet, as stars are fixed in the heavens and are unlikely to hover over towns. The Magi may well have been wealthy, not only because of the gifts they brought to the infant Christ but because they could command an audience with King Herod; it is for this reason that they are described as 'kings'. Yet they were caught by the significance of the new comet in the sky and worked out that a special king had been born. They instinctively knew that this was not the birth of another heir to a secular throne, even though they described Jesus to Herod as 'one who has been born king of the Jews' (Matthew 2:2). This child was not a prince waiting through the course of years to stand in the place of his father. He was already king, and so there must be some new dimension to his rule. The Magi came to worship, not to congratulate!

It is now that the story begins to take its dark and sinister turning. The one with whom the Magi share their news is no less than King Herod the Great. We might think that their approach to him was reckless as well as tactless, to say the least! They might have assumed, however, that the divine child who had been born was a descendant of Herod himself, because they first went to Jerusalem to complete their search.

Herod's own story is complex but there is no doubting his capacity to be ruthless, and determined to keep his throne. He had been married ten times, and over the years had murdered his third wife Mariamne and her mother Alexandra. He had executed three of his sons and imprisoned another, and had written six wills because he could not be sure which sons to favour. He had come to power as king only with the help of Rome, and consolidated his hold by executing 45 members of the Sadducean aristocracy who opposed his rule. All rivals were eliminated, including the high priest in Jerusalem who happened to be his brother-in-law. At the heart of his insecurity and therefore his ruthlessness was the fact that he was an Idumean, a half-Jew who was considered the puppet of Rome and not a true son of David's line. Imagine his consternation, then, at hearing that a new king of the Jews had been born, and that this had been heralded by the appearance of his personal star.

Herod's first reaction was to be disturbed to such a degree that the effects reverberated throughout the city of Jerusalem. The city was weary of the tantrums of Herod that resulted, literally, in bodies in the street. The king may have feared for his throne, and so his initial reaction is very understandable. He went into private consultation with his advisers, the chief priests and scribes, the Sanhedrin consisting of the 72 men who had charge of the civil and religious life of the nation. He wanted to know what the messianic timetable was and in particular where the Messiah was to be born. He was informed that, according to the prophecy of Micah (5:2), the Messiah was to come from the community of Bethlehem, the very same town in which King David had been born. Whether Herod believed the prophecy is not the real point of this story. More important is the fact that almost immediately he began devising a way to eliminate this possible threat to his dynasty.

Herod calls the Magi to a private consultation and is particularly eager to know the exact time that the star first appeared; this is so that he can determine the age of the child, assuming that he was born when the star first appeared. He uses the Magi as decoys to try to locate the actual address of the possible usurper, but disguises his real intentions by pretending to want to follow in their footsteps and worship the Messiah. This could have seemed plausible to the Magi, because one of Herod's claims to fame was his meticulous rebuilding of the temple in Jerusalem. As they set out for Bethlehem on the final leg of their journey, they were not to know that they were serving the murderous intentions of a desperate and ageing despot.

So the Magi are thrilled when the star reappears before them and leads them to the exact spot where this mysterious baby lies. They worship before him and give their gifts, presented as tokens of respect and homage due to a king of the Jews. Frankincense is a highly fragrant incense which was commonly used in worship as a burnt offering to God, while myrrh is a very bitter resin that was used for embalming or preserving, as well as being an ingredient of holy ointment (Exodus 30:23). These would have been very valuable gifts and worthy of a king at this time in history. As Christians we can easily see them as having a deeper significance: we understand the gold to symbolize divine character and worth; frankincense reminds us of our call to recognize and worship Jesus as our king; and myrrh was a prophetic symbol that the child would suffer the bitterness of our sins in order to preserve us through salvation for eternal life.

No doubt the Magi were overjoyed at the completion of their pilgrimage and prepared to return to the East feeling satisfied and content. They had one more duty to perform and that was to inform King Herod of their discovery, as promised. From this duty they were to be rudely shaken in a dream.

Learning the dream message

We are not told what the actual dream conversation was, only that it was a warning and that that the Magi should avoid at all costs giving Herod details of Jesus' exact whereabouts. They may already have had their suspicions; if so, the dream would have come as confirmation. It is encouraging to realize that God knows our circumstances and is well able to deliver his people from danger, provided that we are ready to listen to him. Warning dreams are rather like prophecies in that they can bring the mind of God to us. They should always be prayed over and, if the dream connects with our known circumstances, we should look into the matter to see if the warning has any merit. The Magi's dream is not just a warning, however, but an experience of discernment. With the help of God they see through the façade of Herod's faked humility and discover the real intentions of his heart.

Following the dream

Because the Magi studied dreams, they would have had no difficulty in realizing that this message was genuine. No doubt they would immediately have feared for their own lives, and so we can only guess at the precautions they must have taken in returning home as fast as possible and by a totally different route. For all we know, they may have gone into Egypt, or headed for the coast and taken a boat to safety. Now they disappear from the Christmas story, but in so doing they set in motion a chain of events that happen with great speed. They may have informed Joseph and Mary of their dream, because almost immediately Joseph receives another warning dream on the heels of the one given to the Magi. Joseph and Mary pack their bags and head for relative safety in Egypt. This was to be the only time when Jesus was absent from the land of his birth and the scene of his future ministry and Passion. It is interesting to note that the former land of bondage for the Israelite nation became a land of refuge for the saviour of the world. We are not sure, but this exile may have lasted for anything up to four years.

As so often in life, what was a triumph of grace for one family became a time of murder and mourning for many others. Herod was determined to eradicate the threat to his power, so when he realized that he had been tricked by the Magi he gave orders to kill every male child two years old and under in Bethlehem. Yet not even the ruthlessness of tyrants can prevent the will of God from being carried out, and we should all take hope in this when things seem to go wrong in our lives and ministry. This is just the time to look up to God, not down in despair.

The family's exile does not last for ever, and once again Joseph is told in his sleep what is to be the next step: the tyrant is dead and so they can return in safety to their homeland. It was common knowledge, though, that Archelaus was now on the throne— his father Herod's son and just as dangerous. For example, he slaughtered 3000 people at one of the Passover celebrations in Jerusalem and his rule was so cruel that the Roman emperor had him banished to Gaul after nine years of his rule. Consequently the holy family went to live in Nazareth in Galilee, ruled by another of Herod's sons, Herod Antipas, who was less dangerous to them.

We can only marvel at the way in which God showed up each time the family needed guidance and we can also be impressed by the way in which their warning dreams were so swiftly acted upon. Joseph's actions saved their lives. Imagine if he had ignored his dreams completely or treated them as the result of something he had eaten or drunk the night before! There may have been a dead saviour in Bethlehem and no Christmas story to rejoice in. All these dreams were given for one ultimate purpose, which was to save Jesus so that he could fulfil his role as saviour of the world.

Making it personal

The Christmas warning dreams are all focused on deliverance from evil. To some extent, we could understand them as a recurring dream theme, largely given to Joseph, who seemed to be remarkably receptive to God speaking to him in this kind of way. Without his faith and quick action, humanly speaking, Jesus might well have been killed. I believe that God has not radically altered the ways in which he speaks to us and that we should therefore reconsecrate our dream lives to him and be prepared to hear from God even when we sleep. When I first began to speak on dreams and visions some 25 years ago, many people thought that I was a little 'strange', or even bordering on heretical. The spiritual climate is beginning to change, however, and many more Christians are beginning to realize that dreams are an orthodox resource for us in our lives. I have been so encouraged by the number of Christians who are taking this subject seriously. To give an example of one, I would recommend the book *A Dream Come True* by James Ryle, who is the pastor of a Vineyard church in Boulder, Colorado. If we can be open to this other resource for God to use, we might just begin to hear from him much more than we do at the moment. And who knows? It may just help us to save someone who cannot save themselves.

Prayer

Lord Jesus Christ,
holder of the heavens
who spoke creation into life;
there was a time when you could not speak.
You have been down my path before me.

Lord Jesus Christ,
walker among angels
who rescued the bruised and bewildered;
there was a time when you were carried.
You have been down my path before me.

Lord Jesus Christ,
robed in majesty, crowned,
whose cross is an open triumph;
there was a time when you were hidden.
You have been down my path before me.

When I am speechless, be my living word;
when I cannot stand, be my loving carrier;
when I run and hide, be my loving seeker.
Amen

13

Nightmare Jesus

The trouble with Pilate's wife

———•◦•———

'I had a terrible nightmare about *Jesus* last night.'
Matthew 27:19 (NLT, word in italics mine)

The dream

Just then, as Pilate was sitting on the judgment seat, his wife
sent him this message, 'Leave that innocent man alone, because
I had a terrible nightmare about him last night.'
Matthew 27:19 (NLT)

This was undoubtedly a nightmare. The Collins Concise English
Dictionary defines a nightmare as 'a terrifying or deeply distressing
dream'. This seems to fit the description of the dream that Pilate's
wife presents. Most therapists agree that nightmares relate to
two aspects of our lives. One is those fears and disturbing feelings
that reflect deep impulses and drives about which we are still
uncomfortable or unsure. The second is objective experiences
from either our childhood or more recent events which have
left a deep and upsetting impression upon us. Most people in the
course of their lifetimes have at least one nightmare that they
remember, along with the impression that such dreams have made
upon them.

Most nightmares have a recognizable pattern. They make an
intense, if not frightening and disturbing, impression upon us,
and just before the 'nasty' climax happens we wake up, bailing
out of the dream—only to have it again another time. This gives
us some insights to the nature of nightmares. The first is that we

are largely in control of our dreams, because we can stop them when they become too disturbing. Second, because we stall the dream and prevent it from finishing its course, we usually have it again until it is somehow completed. Finally, all nightmares are about one fundamental issue in our lives—unfinished business. They concern business that is either too threatening or too distasteful for us to acknowledge and work through.

If it is true that we are largely in control of our dreams, then we could well ask, 'Why do we want to frighten ourselves when we sleep?' I was confronted with this question when I was leading a dream workshop in Bradford Cathedral a few years ago. My reply rather stunned the questioner, because I said that a nightmare is seven-eighths of a healing story. What I meant by this is that the dream is of our own making; we are owning something that has had a profound effect upon us and we have almost finished the story, but we have not worked through to an ending. When people are able to finish their nightmare journey, they can complete something that they have been working through or wrestling with, and move on into more wholeness in their lives. Pilate's wife was deeply upset by her dream and it had something to do with Jesus. By working it through, she could perhaps come to a place of healing about Jesus. Before we can appreciate what this meant for her, we need to understand what led to her having this terrifying dream in the first place.

The story behind the dream

The backdrop to the nightmare was the drama unfolding over the plot to put Jesus to death. It was a hastily conceived conspiracy, led by Caiaphas the high priest, with some of the religious and secular leaders in Jerusalem. They secured the help of Judas, one of Jesus' disciples who, for reasons we are not told, was disaffected with his master and so agreed to betray him. He told the conspirators where and when to capture their quarry (Matthew 26:1–5, 14–16). Consequently, in the early hours of the morning, Judas led an armed mob into the prayer meeting that Jesus was leading in the garden of Gethsemane, and arrested him (Matthew 26:47–56). Jesus was given a mock trial inside the house of Caiaphas, where false witnesses fell over themselves in an unsuccessful attempt to prove his guilt. Eventually they accused him of blasphemy because he identified himself as the divine son of God, and they bundled him over to the praetorium to face Pilate, the Roman governor. They hoped that Pilate would rubber-stamp their judgment and carry out the execution of the man they hated so much (Matthew 26:57–67; 27:1–2).

So the stage is set and the trial is just under way when a servant comes up to Pilate to tell him of his wife's nightmare. Now, for a brief moment in time that still speaks powerfully to us today, three people are locked into a moment of dream sharing that will to a large degree decide their future, depending upon their responses. First there is Pilate's wife, who is mentioned here for the first and only time in the entire New Testament. We do not even know her name. It was the writers of the apocryphal Gospels who first suggested that she was Claudia Procula, a member of the imperial household, the youngest daughter of Julia, daughter of Augustus, who had married Tiberius as her second husband. This could explain why she accompanied her husband Pilate to Judea during his time as governor there: it was usually forbidden for wives to join their husbands as they were considered a security risk. She must have had some kind of independence in order to leave the governor's palace in Caesarea and accompany her husband to Jerusalem, which would have been regarded as unsafe and dangerous. There is not much more we can say about her although, with the passage of time, she has been canonized in both the Greek and Coptic churches, and in Ethiopia her feast day is 25 June.

The second person in our trio is Pilate himself. He had been governor of Judea for approximately six years when he conducted Jesus' trial, so he was no novice concerning the culture and religious practices of the people he ruled. He appears in the Gospel story only during the trial of Jesus and yet his name has been immortalized in the Christian creeds. He was recalled to Rome, presumably in disgrace, in AD 36 and is heard of no more. He may well have been executed in the purges of Tiberius following the downfall of Sejanus who, some scholars believe, gave Pilate his post in Judea. By all accounts he was a complex man and could be ruthless when he wanted to be. Luke records that he murdered some Galileans during the feast of Passover and this could explain why he and Herod Antipas, the ruler of Galilee, were enemies at this time (Luke 13:1; 23:12). For a brilliant analysis of Pilate and his life, I recommend Ann Wroe's wonderful book, *Pilate: the biography of an invented man.*[1]

When Pilate is told about his wife's nightmare, the trial is already under way. He had listened to the religious arguments and accusations made against Jesus, and was clearly not impressed by them. Apparently he knew that the real motive behind the trial was the envy of the Jewish leaders over Jesus' power and popularity, which suggests that Pilate had some knowledge of what Jesus was doing and the effect he was having upon the religious climate of the territory (Matthew 27:18). We can only guess whether this had formed part of the discussion that he must have had with his wife about Jesus.

The crucial moment of the trial has arrived: Pilate has offered the crowd the choice between releasing Barabbas, a convicted murderer awaiting execution, or Jesus, victim of the rage of the high priests (Matthew 27:15–18). Pilate sits down in the judgment seat and awaits their choice; and this is the moment when the servant brings in news of his wife's dream. It is the moment of decision but, before the decision is made, a dream interrupts the proceedings. Matthew is the only Gospel writer to record this episode, but we must not be tempted into thinking that it is therefore invention. We have already noted how exceptional it was for a Roman official to be accompanied by his wife on an overseas posting and that this points to the determination and influence of the woman concerned. We shouldn't be surprised that, if she felt so strongly about something, then she would think nothing of interrupting her husband during his work hours to tell him about it.

The third person in this moment of dream sharing is the almost silent Jesus, bound, blindfolded and beaten by the guards. With accusations flying all around him, he has not answered one of them, even though Pilate has remarked on his silence. He has neither defended himself nor asked for mercy—and this impressed Pilate, who must have confronted hundreds of condemned men (Matthew 27:12–14). In some mysterious way, these two men have become entwined in each other's destinies—Jesus the silent one and Pilate the cynical and powerful ruler. Pilate must have received the message that he did not impress Jesus one bit, and surely it bothered him that this was so. All four Gospels mention how the governor asked Jesus if he was king of the Jews. When Jesus concurred, Pilate tried to have him released. It is almost as if Pilate needed to demonstrate his ability to do something for Jesus' welfare. It is an amazing thing that the bound and apparently powerless Christ could still unnerve the mighty. Jesus is still making people uncomfortable when they are faced with his uncompromising innocence and love.

In mid-trial, therefore, Pilate, his wife and Jesus stand confronted with a nightmare which is blunt and to the point. I often wonder how Jesus felt when he heard the dream, which was all about him, spelled out by the servant to the man who had to make his mind up what to do about it. We cannot know if he felt some measure of strengthening to hear his name mentioned in a kindly way at the very moment when the mob was screaming for his crucifixion. However, it has been the kind words and actions of friends that have helped me face my dark times and work them through in the hope of a good end.

Learning the dream message

The startling message in the nightmare is that Jesus is innocent. The actual word used in the text means 'righteous' and refers to the legal status of being 'not guilty' of a crime. Pilate's wife is clear in her intentions: she wants her husband to release Jesus. The obvious question to ask is how she knows that Jesus is innocent.

Was she a secret disciple? One of the early Church Fathers, Origen, thought that she was the first Gentile to believe in Jesus' teaching and described her as 'the proselyte of the Gate'.[2] The Greeks and Copts even put her among the women who went to the tomb to pray. We can only surmise that she had heard about Jesus from the gossip of the court, or heard the rumours about him that were gripping the people of Jerusalem: the fact that he had flogged the money changers in the temple could not have escaped her attention or that of her husband. Did she come in disguise to hear him preach on the open hills? Had she slipped into the back of the synagogue to hear him talk, or did she see him heal the sick? All this is speculation, but we have to account for the fact that she was greatly disturbed in her dream in some way and that she knew that Jesus was innocent. Something must have convinced her of this. Rather than the nightmare being a bolt from the blue, it is more likely that she had been impressed by Jesus and had heard the whispers and intrigue surrounding his arrest. It all boiled over in her mind, and before she finished the dream, with its bloody climax of crucifixion, she was startled awake and determined to act. The Jesus in her nightmare had to be saved. She was determined to tell this to Pilate—but would he listen?

Following the dream

It was unthinkable that a governor's wife should enter the judgment hall in the middle of a trial, and so the unnamed servant is sent. Interestingly enough, he tells the dream as if Pilate's wife herself is speaking. This suggests that he might have been reading it out aloud from a sealed letter that he had been given. Claudia Procula at least tried to do something about her dream message: she followed it through as best she could. Pilate would undoubtedly have given some credence to the dream, as dreams were recognized as a vehicle for divine warnings in times of crisis. Both Julius Caesar and his wife Calpurnia had had disturbing dreams on the night before he was assassinated on the steps of the Roman Senate, and there was a popular book called *Memorable Sayings and Doings*, by Valerius Maximus, circulating in Roman society at this time. It described many such warning dreams that had affected the great and the good, and they were either delivered or doomed according to whether they heeded the warnings or not.

It is clear from the biblical accounts that Pilate begins to show signs of agitation and anxiety from this moment onwards throughout the trial. He keeps getting up, pacing up and down, and going in and out of the praetorium. Ann Wroe points out that such turbulence had no place in a trial; if the crime was serious, Pilate should have judged it sitting utterly still on his judgment seat, the sacred symbol of justice and of his office.[3] Instead he was full of unease. It is obvious that the dream message had had its desired effect. Luke's version of the trial at this point describes Pilate saying that he could find nothing wrong with the accused man (Luke 23:4). In fact, Luke relates two further moments when Pilate tried to free Jesus but was defeated by the determination of the mob to crucify their prisoner (Luke 23:16, 22). John's version goes deeper into the complexity of Pilate's heart by pointing out that even when Jesus was robed, crowned with thorns and on his way to execution, the governor none the less pronounced him not guilty! (John 19:4, 6).

However, when the mob, whipped up by the chief priests, yells out that Jesus should be crucified, Pilate begins to crumble. They prefer Barabbas to Jesus, and Pilate begins to feel that he is being trapped by his own attempts to be generous to Jesus. The mob is in danger of rioting, and among the threats of violence is a veiled threat to Pilate himself. Someone cries out, 'If you release this man you are not a friend to Caesar. Anyone who declares himself a king is a rebel against Caesar' (John 19:12, NLT). In those turbulent times, when plots and intrigue surrounded the imperial house of Tiberius, it was not uncommon for those suspected of treason to be executed without trial and Pilate would have known this. Therefore, like many a person faced with the cost of being true and honest, he decided to side with the crowd and save himself from possible harm. It is now that Pilate judges Jesus but he is clearly not happy to do so. He washes his hands in public—but this action would not have impressed the mob in the least. It serves more as a private ritual to appease his own conscience. Pilate declares himself innocent and passes the responsibility for the act of execution over to the accusers (Matthew 27:24). Strictly speaking, this is a piece of nonsense, because Pilate as governor was the judge and jury that day: the real responsibility was his. But it was his conscience that he was trying to clear. So Jesus is flogged, dressed up as a clown king and sent out to his death on the cross.

Making it personal

In an interview in the *Sunday Telegraph*, a year before becoming Prime Minister, Tony Blair said:

> The intriguing thing about Pilate is the degree to which he tried to do the good thing rather than the bad. He commands our moral attention not because he was a bad man, but because he was so nearly a good man. One can imagine him agonizing, seeing that Jesus had done nothing wrong, and wishing to release him. Just as easily, however, one can envisage Pilate's advisers telling him of the risks, warning him not to cause a riot or inflame Jewish opinion. It is a timeless parable of political life . . . Christianity is optimistic about the human condition, but not naive. It can identify what is good, but knows the capacity to do evil. I believe that the endless striving to do the one and avoid the other is the purpose of human existence. Through that, progress comes.[4]

We may all have our stories about when we failed to do the right thing, but few of us will have experienced so public a failure as that of Pilate. He has been remembered ever since as the man who judged the saviour of the world. The early sermons preached by the apostles mention Pilate and are clearly aware of his dithering over decisions. When Peter preached at the temple after healing the lame man, he spoke of Pilate's decision to release Jesus being overruled by the mob (Acts 3:13). Later on, after his own brush with the Council, Peter decried Pilate as being in a conspiracy with Herod Antipas, Gentiles and the people of Israel in their determination to execute Jesus (Acts 4:28).

We have seen only a glimpse of the inner struggles of Pilate, which were sparked to some degree by his wife's nightmare. This is not an attempt to excuse him, but a plea for understanding for the fallen. Many of us have made bad decisions because we did not have friends to stand beside us and support us in the times when we wrestled over what action to take. Perhaps we can be a friend to others who are struggling with truth, strengthening them to do the right thing when faced with a difficult choice.

Finally, we can see that Claudia Procula's dream, though deeply upsetting to her, was in fact a word from God to recognize truth and live in its light This she clearly tried to do. When we have disturbing dreams like hers, we should resist the urge simply to write them off as a bad dream, or even one in which we feel attacked by some kind of dark spirit. Just because a dream is disturbing, it does not mean that it is bad. The dream may be a way of trying to get to grips with something that really hurts or bothers us. It may be an unfinished healing story, waiting for us to work through the closing chapter and face up to what frightens or threatens us. As a way of preparing to unpack a dream like this, prayerfully share it with a friend. Do not immediately try to interpret it or try to give meaning to the symbols. Invite Jesus into your dream picture and see how he will interact with the story you have been sharing. It is just like writing the final chapter to a novel that you have been working on in your sleep. You are still the writer, even though you are now awake to go through the final portion. This pictorial, storytelling way of working with Jesus at the centre of a nightmare can often help us to face up to what is bothering us—in the power and presence of the risen Christ, who once listened to a nightmare being shared at his own time of trial.

Prayer

Wild Spirit of the living God,
be the calm in my storm,
the light in my dark;
the One who believes in me
even when I don't.

Warm Son of the loving Father,
the healer of my hurts,
the holder of my hands;
who seeks better things for me
even when I can't,
light the lion's flame of passion in my life,
give me the giving heart of heaven's holy warrior,
so that I learn to be still,
to be stopped,
to recover,
to be released
and renewed
through Jesus Christ,
my Lord and victorious lamb.
Amen

14

The man for the moment

Ananias' gift to world mission

So Ananias went and found the house, placed his hands on blind Saul, and said, 'Brother Saul, the Master sent me, the same Jesus you saw on the way here.'

Acts 9:17 (The Message)

The dream

Now there was a believer in Damascus named Ananias. The Lord spoke to him in a vision, calling 'Ananias!' 'Yes, Lord!' he replied. The Lord said, 'Go over to Straight Street, to the house of Judas. When you arrive, ask for Saul of Tarsus. He is praying to me right now. I have shown him a vision of a man named Ananias coming and laying hands on him so that he can see again.' 'But Lord,' exclaimed Ananias, 'I've heard about the terrible things this man has done to believers in Jerusalem! And we hear that he is authorized by the leading priests to arrest every believer in Damascus.' But the Lord said, 'Go and do what I say. For Saul is my chosen instrument to take my message to the Gentiles and to the kings, as well as to the people of Israel. And I will show him how much he must suffer for me.'

Acts 9:10–16 (NLT)

This is a story of two visions in one day, one experienced by the future apostle Paul, perhaps the most famous Christian, and the other by Ananias, a relatively unknown Christian who steps from obscurity to perform one of the most crucial acts of faith and then disappears from history. We have already seen in Chapter 8 how visions are used by God to alert us to his purposes and call his people into ministry. Throughout the Bible, dreams and visions seem to be parallel experiences that can occur at the same time. The Hebrew word for dream is *harlam* and, like its Aramaic counterpart, means 'to make whole or healthy'. Instantly this should alert us to the fact that one of the functions of dreaming in scripture is to help us to grow in wholeness and integration in our personal lives. Perhaps this is why the psalmist wrote, '(God) grants sleep to those he loves' (Psalm 127:2, NIV). The Hebrew for vision, on the other hand, implies the ability to perceive with the inner eye and, as such, is closely aligned with the word 'seer'. It comes very close to the Greek word for 'dream', which is *honar*, meaning 'to see or envision in sleep'. Thayer's Greek Lexicon defines 'vision' as 'a sudden emotion whereby one is transported as it were out of himself, so that in this rapt condition, although awake, his mind is drawn off from all surrounding objects and so wholly fixed on things divine that he sees nothing but the forms and images lying within, and thinks that he perceives with his bodily eyes and ears realities shown him by God'.[1] I think, however, that this is a flawed understanding of vision within scripture. Naturally, spiritual experiences are going to affect our emotions, sometimes quite powerfully, but there is no reason to think that this also means the loss of awareness of our circumstances or even of our reason. As we shall see, Ananias was well able to discuss with God the real life circumstances to which the vision related, and even argue about it.

Morton T. Kelsey tries to pinpoint the differences between dreams and visions by saying that a dream is the mode or expression of the experience while a vision is the content or substance of what is experienced.[2] This seems an unnecessarily laborious way of trying to show how dreams and visions differ. It is much simpler to say that dreams are normally contained within sleep whereas visions can happen both when we are awake and when we are asleep. Another distinction is that we are normally the creators of our dreams and that it is God who gives visions. However, there are times when the two things happen at the same time, and this is normally during sleep. There are two expressions in the Bible that relate to this experience. The first is 'vision of the night' (Genesis 46:2; Job 20:8; 33:15; Isaiah 29:7; Daniel 2:19; 7:2, 7, 13; Acts 16:9; 18:9) and the second is 'vision in my head' (Daniel 2:28; 4:5, 10, 13). In all of these cases, the vision material concerns the personal reflections of the sleeper and his current predicament in life. So we can say that in these cases the dreamer is asleep, creating a dream story or comment, and into this piece of personal creativity God comes and weaves into the dream material an agenda of his own.

It is not clear whether Ananias was asleep when he had his vision but, as we have seen, this really does not matter. As we shall see, the message that God was about to bring him was already on his mind. He needed no vision to know about Saul of Tarsus.

The story behind the dream

It was a time of increasing persecution of the Jewish Christians, and the most prominent leader of this murderous movement was Saul of Tarsus. He was present when Stephen, the first Christian martyr, was stoned to death in Jerusalem. Saul is described as one who approved of the killing (Acts 7:58; 8:1). It is possible that he was impressed by Stephen's witness because Luke says that the martyr's appearance was like the face of an angel and that the Council members couldn't take their eyes off him but stared at him with astonishment (Acts 6:15). When the moment of Stephen's death came, he died with similar words on his lips to those of the dying Jesus: 'Lord Jesus, receive my spirit . . . don't charge them with this sin' (Acts 7:59–60). It was not a judicial execution, it was the fury of the mob unleashed on a single victim. Members of the Council lost their composure and rushed at Stephen, forcibly dragging him from the court to somewhere outside the walls of Jerusalem and stoning him until he was dead (Acts 7:57–58). This was mob violence and it satisfied Saul. It sparked off a wave of persecutions around the city and into the countryside, as far afield as Damascus in Syria.

At the heart of this pogrom was Saul, who is described as keeping up his violent threats of murder against the followers of the Lord (Acts 9:1, GNB). He spared no one. Men, women and presumably children too were to be shackled with chains and dragged back to Jerusalem for trial. Saul was no doubt a devout Jew and a Pharisee, and may even have been a member of the Sanhedrin (Philippians 3:4–6). Yet his rage at the Church seems to have gone deeper than his zeal for the *Torah* and suggests that he was wrestling with an inner turmoil or conviction from God that had powerfully spoken to him through the witness of Stephen.

It is true for many of us that if we find something that is true and good, we often rebel against it because it threatens our current way of life. We try to destroy its influence over us in a bid to regain peace of mind. It was this inner battle that wracked Saul's heart as he headed out towards Damascus in search of more upstart Christians. It was going to be a journey into destiny and transformation.

Just outside the city, Saul was stopped in his tracks by the very one he opposed—Jesus himself. A brilliant light shone from heaven and Jesus asked Saul why he was persecuting him. Saul gave no answer; he just asked who it was that was speaking from heaven. It must have been a severe shock to him to be told that it was Jesus, because Saul had dismissed him as an impostor. In that moment he took a quantum leap of conversion; he saw the truth and was physically blinded by it (Acts 9:3–9). It was a profound and disturbing face-to-face encounter with Jesus, and it is no wonder that Saul couldn't eat or do anything for three days, but simply pray and repent. This is a reminder to us not to paint conversion to Christ as a picnic, something that can happen without effort or problems. It can be very costly and upsetting, because it is an almost complete reversal in our priorities and commitment; we may well have much to lose, so that our conversion can be a kind of grief journey. It was C.S. Lewis who described, in his autobiography *Surprised by Joy*, his coming to faith in Christ as the birth of a reluctant baby who came kicking and screaming into the world. Saul was broken and utterly exhausted by the change of direction in his life. He needed help, and it was about to come from a man he had briefly glimpsed in a vision of his own.

Learning the dream message

The vision of Ananias is a truly startling one and it reminds us of how utterly able our God is to guide the affairs of people. First he calls Ananias by name. This was not just to get his attention but also to establish that God wanted to relate to him personally; he could have sent an angel as on other occasions, but God made this contact very personal indeed. Then Ananias must have been stunned by the detail of the message that came. He was to go to a particular address in Damascus, the house of Judas which was on Straight Street, the main arterial road that ran right through the centre of the town. It may have been an address known to him. In this house lay the most dangerous man in Syria, as far as Ananias was concerned, and he was being commanded to go and lay hands on him in order to heal his blindness! God encouraged him by saying that Saul himself, even though he was blinded, had had a vision of Ananias coming to pray for him and heal him. Though he could not physically see, he could see in his mind's eye what his helper looked like and what he would do. Astounding! But had Ananias ever done this before? Was he known for his healing ministry or his practice of miraculous gifts? This does not appear to be the case. Paul described him later as a man known for his godliness and love of the *Torah* and in good standing with the Jews in the community (Acts 22:12). It may have been this latter factor that helped to build the bridge into Saul's heart, allowing him to be open to the healing that God had for him. These are the only references to Ananias, who stepped out of obscurity and became the man for the moment.

Ananias also needed help, however. He had heard about Saul and was afraid. Perhaps this is why God told him that Saul was praying and not still persecuting. Ananias protested that it was too dangerous to go. It is worth pointing out that even though he was having a vision, his ability to rationalize and argue with God had not been suspended. However, God insisted that he must go and, in order to help him make up his mind, he revealed more of his plans to Ananias. God told this unknown disciple that he was preparing Saul for his ministry to Gentiles, to kings and also to the people of Israel. Ananias was the first to be told that the gospel was actually intended by God to break out of its boundaries within the Jewish people and reach everyone. This was radically new and it was first announced to someone who would probably not be involved in carrying it out. Yet, without Ananias, Christianity might have stayed in relative obscurity within Judaism and might even have fizzled out before too long. And there was something else: God revealed that Saul was going to suffer many things for Jesus, and this must have impressed Ananias. Perhaps it softened his heart, but he did not mention it when he eventually went to meet Saul; this was something only God could reveal to Saul when the right time came. Ananias was about to make a brief appearance on the public stage which would have the deepest effect on the rest of the world, although he would hardly have known it at the time.

Following the dream

Who knows what was going through Ananias' mind as he walked down Straight Street and came to the house where the former persecutor was staying? Whatever his misgivings, as soon as he was shown into the room with the blinded Saul he uttered words that would have come as a welcome relief to Saul. Ananias called him 'brother Saul'. (Acts 9:17). The former persecutor and killer of Christians was now a member of the church family and to be welcomed accordingly. It was an amazing step of humility and faith by Ananias, and the fact that Paul later referred to him more than once is proof of how profoundly he had been blessed by their meeting. Saul had had a vision of this man coming and praying with him, but Ananias' words must have come as healing touches that went deep. Ananias explained that the Lord Jesus who had appeared to Saul on the road had also told him, Ananias, to come and minister so that Saul would be healed. He laid hands on Saul and immediately Saul's sight was restored. Ananias did not stop there. He prayed for the infilling of the Holy Spirit and he baptized Saul in water (Acts 9:18).

I find it so touching that the unknown servants of God, for a brief moment in time, lay their hands on those who will become effective and influential over nations. Without the ordinary Christians like Ananias, I suspect that the kingdom of God would be very poor indeed and not nearly so advanced in the purposes of God as it is.

Ananias must have done something else, although it is not directly recorded. He probably introduced Saul to other Christians in the city, because Saul stayed with them for a while and, with their help, began his public preaching in the synagogue (Acts 9:19–20). Ananias gave Saul fellowship and support and it was from these basic beginnings, the gifts of a relatively unknown disciple who never appears on the public stage again, that Saul went on to become the greatest missionary and theologian of his day. He turned his part of the world upside down and, through his writings, has reached countless millions down the centuries ever since.

Making it personal

Saul of Tarsus had a vision of help coming his way and all he had to do was to wait for it. Ananias had a vision to go and help somebody and all he had to do was to act upon it. There are times in our lives when we have to learn to be patient and wait for God to act, not trying to force a thing to happen. Waiting on God is something that we are bad at in our age of instant meals and communications. We are tempted to think that nothing is happening and find it hard to believe that God is at work. Yet often it is in the waiting times of our lives that we are drawn into deeper intimacy with God—and this is his prime goal for us, because he is far more concerned about what he can do *in* our lives than what he can do *with* our lives. No doubt, racing through Saul's heart was a stream of reflections about what his rage and zeal had achieved for him. Perhaps his conscience played on him as he began to realize the damage he had been doing and how he had been trying to eradicate the impression that the martyr Stephen had made upon him. He knew deep down that he had been fighting against the risen Jesus, because when he was challenged on the road to Damascus he knew instinctively that he was speaking to his Lord. No wonder he spent his blinded moments praying. This was the beginning of transformation, when his lost life was recovered and he found new direction for his energies. He emerged from this ordeal as a man with a mission in life and he never allowed himself to be deflected from it. It all came out of waiting on God for the help and resources he needed. Within days he was preaching powerfully in the city. Our days of waiting can be the most productive in our lives as God renews the vision he has for us and the developing ministry that will come out of our deepening relationship with him.

Ananias, in contrast, was challenged in a vision to act. In doing so he had to face his fears and defeat them by trust in God. His major gift of ministry was to welcome an outcast into the fellowship of Christ and, in so doing, release an immense ministry far beyond his own capabilities. He may never have done anything else as significant after this, but the fruit of his sharing was incalculable for the advance of the kingdom of God.

The encouragement for us is not to withhold our gift—whether great or small—from others. Who knows what blessings it may bring? Philip left a scene of amazing miracles of healing and revival in Samaria and followed the Spirit's guidance to a desert highway on the Gaza strip (Acts 8:26–40). We might have thought that this was a waste of a gifted evangelist, yet there he met a court official on his way home to Ethiopia and shared the gospel with this one person. History records that a strong Christian church grew in Ethiopia, which is still flourishing to this day. When Jesus entered the upper room in Jerusalem for the second time after his resurrection, he came to transform the one person who had not been there before—Thomas. He encouraged Thomas to touch him and believe in the resurrection (John 20:24–29). Tradition tells us that Thomas went on to become an effective missionary in India. His individual encounter with Christ healed the depressing doubt of his heart, firing him with new passion for his Lord so that he went on to serve him with distinction. Closer to our time, a diminutive religious sister, born in Albania, felt called by God to serve the poorest of the poor and weak. From her step of faith, Mother Teresa's work with the most helpless became known around the world. At one time she was quizzed by Malcolm Muggeridge, who thought that her work was admirable but a waste of talent. 'Why do you give your time to caring for people who die within hours of bringing them into your hospitals?' he asked. Her reply was memorable. She said it was true that the majority of the patients did die quite soon afterwards, but they died with dignity and not as garbage cast out by society. This was one of the miracles of caring that changed the cynical journalist to start searching for salvation for himself.

No matter how little or ordinary we might think we are, if we put ourselves into the hands of Jesus, he can bring from our lives great things for God. Let us be bold in listening to the word of the Lord for our lives and learn to step out in faith and offer what we have, in the belief that Jesus can make something beautiful for God from it.

Prayer

Wild Spirit of the living God,
give me the eye of the eagle,
so that I can see what is far off
and live in its truth, here and now.
Amen

15

Windows on the world

Peter's rooftop dream

―――――•‐◆‐•―――――

The voice spoke to him again, 'Do not consider anything unclean that God has declared clean.'   *Acts 10:15 (GNB)*

The dream

The next day, as they were on their way and coming near Joppa, Peter went up on the roof of the house about noon in order to pray. He became hungry and wanted something to eat; while the food was being prepared, he had a vision. He saw heaven opened and something coming down that looked like a large sheet being lowered by its four corners to the earth. In it were all kinds of animals, reptiles and wild birds. A voice said to him, 'Get up, Peter; kill and eat!' But Peter said, 'Certainly not, Lord! I have never eaten anything ritually unclean or defiled.' The voice spoke to him again, 'Do not consider anything unclean that God has declared clean.' This happened three times, and then the thing was taken back up into heaven.   *Acts 10:9–16 (GNB)*

Although the scriptures do not say it overtly, Peter was more than likely daydreaming on a rooftop with the smell of cooking food wafting up to him from the kitchens below. It is important to notice this because his ordinary senses were going to become the springboard for God to bring him a vision that would revolutionize his life. This is often God's way with us. As we have seen with Joseph, with the baker and cupbearer, with Pharaoh and King Nebuchadnezzar, God used what was already occupying their minds to become the link to reveal what he planned to do.

There are similarities between Peter's 'trance encounter' with God and the experience of Paul who, as a recent convert to Christianity, was preaching amid mounting hostility in Jerusalem (Acts 22:17–21). With this trouble upon his mind, he went to the temple to pray and God spoke to him in a vision, urging him to leave the city as people were plotting his death. It was at this moment that Paul realized he would have to focus and prioritize his ministry on the Gentile nations.

The word used in the Acts 10 passage for 'vision' is *ekstasis* and it is usually translated as 'ecstasy'. The word means 'to stand outside of oneself' and W. E. Vine defines it as 'a condition in which ordinary consciousness and the perception of the natural circumstances were withheld and the soul was susceptible only to the vision which God imparted'.[1] One moment Peter was relaxing in anticipation of a good meal and the next he was transported to a meal of forbidden food. This vision-picture was presented three times before the interview with God was over. I wonder if this reminded Peter of an earlier encounter with his Lord, when he was asked three times if he loved Jesus more than anything else, until he got the message. This was the encounter with the resurrected Jesus on the lake shore beside the charcoal fire (John 21:9, 15–19). It is interesting to note, by the way, that the word for charcoal fire (*anthrakian*) occurs only twice in the New Testament, but both times they feature in accounts of Peter's relationship with Jesus. The first occasion is during the trial of Jesus at Caiaphas' house, when Peter was questioned three times by various people about whether he was one of Jesus' disciples (John 18:15–27). He denied knowledge of his Lord and this denial cut him to the heart. The second occasion, on the lake shore after the resurrection, was an opportunity to answer each of those stinging denials with an affirmation of love and commitment. No doubt it was a very uncomfortable interview but the outcome was a reinstated and remotivated apostle who became an extraordinary leader in the early Church.

It seems that one of the reasons why God speaks repeatedly into our dreams or presents us with a vision that stays with us is to give us an opportunity to find new direction and healing in our lives. He wants to lead us out of the culs-de-sac we often make for ourselves and into new challenges, in newness of life. This was about to happen to Peter on the rooftop because, as soon as the vision was over, opportunity was knocking at his door to put its message into practice.

The story behind the dream

The action in this story began 25 miles or so away from Joppa, in Caesarea, the capital city of Judea and the headquarters of the Roman governor for the province, It began with a waking vision given to the captain of a Roman regiment whose name was Cornelius. His regiment was called the Italian Regiment, which was probably made up of conscripts from throughout Italy and, more than likely, did not include the usual mixture of soldiers from other countries. There could have been anything from 400 to 600 men in his garrison. Cornelius, therefore, was a man of considerable influence who probably served the Roman governor of the day. He is described as a worshipper of God and a friend to the Jews—no mean feat for a high-ranking officer of an occupying army. He was a man of prayer, and it seems that his household shared his faith and diligence. He is not described as a convert to the Jewish faith, so we can conclude that he was seeking God according to the light he had. It is challenging to accept that it was to this man that God gave the first step towards changing the mind-set of what was, up until this point, a totally Jewish Christian Church. Because of his own openness to God, Cornelius would be indirectly responsible for helping the Church to accept the inclusion of the Gentiles into the body of Christ. Peter would be the key instrument, but he could not have done it without Cornelius' steps of faith. It is so often the way that great things for God are achieved when people take small steps of obedience and offer to God what they consider to be little gifts, setting in motion an amazing trail of mighty things.

Cornelius had a waking vision at about three o'clock in the afternoon and, like Peter, it was in the context of his prayers. He saw an angel enter his house and speak to him (10:1–6). When he had composed himself from the shock of the sight before him, he was given precise information: he was to go to Joppa and seek out Peter, who was in the house of Simon the tanner. Whatever the encounter was going to mean, the angel told Cornelius that it would be the answer to his prayers. This is the real clue as to what was in those prayers. He had been seeking after God in order that his doubts, his questions and his needs would be met and fulfilled. He called some trusted servants, who included another devout soldier like himself, and instructed them to go and find Peter.

The next morning they set out for Joppa, no doubt tingling with anticipation as to what would happen next, and the timing is amazing. Just as they arrive in the town, Peter is on the shaded rooftop, praying. I wonder what was the subject of his prayers. He may have been thinking about the last few days of tremendous healing miracles. A paralysed man called Aeneas had been healed so that he was able to get out of bed for the first time in eight years (Acts 9:32–35). Tabitha, a Jewish Christian in Joppa, had been raised from the dead and the news of it had set the town alight with gossip and wonder (Acts 9:36–43). It may have been this event that helped Cornelius' servants to locate the house where Peter was staying. Perhaps he was praising the Lord because everything was going so well. Or was he thinking of what God had in store for him next?

It was a vision that had set in motion the delegation to Peter's door, and it was going to take another to help Peter to let them in, in more ways than one.

Learning the dream message

Peter's dream consisted of a picture and a command. The picture was of food that Jews considered to be ritually unclean, such as reptiles and wild birds (Leviticus 11:2–27; Deuteronomy 14:3–20).

The command was to eat what had formerly been forbidden. Peter's reaction was the expected one: he refused, with protestations of his devoutness. He keeps to the rules of his faith and he seems determined to say so, no doubt thinking that he was on safe ground with God. How wrong he was! Peter made the classic mistake of replacing God with his rules. These dietary rules were there in the *Torah* but the God who made them was entitled to bend them by grace.

In a sense, Peter shows classic Pharisaism. Jesus had challenged the Pharisees because they had made the Sabbath a matter of rule-keeping and lost the whole point that it was designed for people to enjoy the presence of God (Mark 2:23–28). This is why God confronts Peter, telling him not to call 'unclean' what God himself now pronounces 'clean'. It must have been a confusing time, as all Peter's principles were seemingly being put aside. Peter is baffled, even though the picture and the command come from heaven three times. Then the vision suddenly ends and he is stuck with his mixture of protestations and convictions.

It is easy for us to read this story and understand the symbols because we know what happens next, but we must appreciate that Peter was being asked to make a quantum leap of faith. It was the strangers now at his door who would help him to unravel the puzzle in his mind.

Following the dream

One thing is certain: Peter did not dismiss the dream vision as a consequence of his hungry stomach. He wondered and thought about it and tried to unravel the various conflicting feelings that it gave him. It played on his mind and would not let him go (Acts 10:17, 19). Then the strangers shouted up from the street down below, 'Is there a guest here by the name of Simon Peter?' (Acts 10:18). Peter heard them, and at that moment the Holy Spirit gave him a word of wisdom, telling him to go with these visitors to wherever they came from, and to do so without hesitation or question (Acts 10:19–21). Peter was to trust that God was in the event and to rely on him to work it out well. I imagine that his mind must have been racing with questions and objections! It is a sign of his obedience and maturing faith that he could trust God even when he was battling in his heart about whether he was doing the right thing. It all seemed so unclear and doubtful, and yet he was about to become a key figure in another Pentecost—the outpouring of the Holy Spirit on Gentiles for the very first time. This was to be the moment when the Christian Church ceased to be limited to the Jewish people and started to become the international and multi-ethnic witness that it is today. It all began here, with strangers meeting in the afternoon in a leather worker's house in Joppa (modern-day Jaffa).

Two testimonies were necessary to achieve what God had in mind for the journey to Caesarea and Peter's ministry to Cornelius and his family. The servants and Cornelius himself related to Peter the vision of the angel and his message. Only at this point was Peter able to work out his dream picture and see the spiritual message and importance of it. This is clear from his opening words as he got up to speak: 'I now realize that it is true that God treats everyone on the same basis . . . no matter what race he belongs to' (Acts 10:34–35, GNB). It had been a massive step of faith for Peter just to enter Cornelius' house; in doing so, he was breaking away from all he had been taught about the Gentiles being ritually unclean and inferior. Once he had taken that step, he became the first to preach the gospel to the Gentiles just as he had been the first to preach to his fellow Jews (Acts 10:36–43). As he was still preaching, the Holy Spirit fell on all of them and the Gentile Pentecost was under way. They spoke in tongues and praised God just like the disciples in the upper room had done on the first day of Pentecost. For Peter, this was the convincing manifestation that the Gentiles were now members of the Church and so he didn't hesitate to baptize them with water to signify it (Acts 10:46–48). He later used it to justify his actions to the church leaders in Jerusalem, who doubted the wisdom of what he had done (Acts 11:1–18).

Incidentally, this episode should encourage us to recognize the healing value of speaking in tongues. However this gift has been misused through history, according to scripture one of its prime effects is to unite people who would not normally be in harmony. On the first day of Pentecost, scattered Jews from all over Asia were united in hearing the witness of the disciples to the resurrection of Jesus, because it was sounded out in the streets through gifts of tongues (Acts 2:1–11). In Cornelius' house, Peter and his own companions were convinced and united with their new friends in Christ when they heard them speaking in tongues.

It would be impossible to underestimate the importance of this step in the life of the Christian Church. Once taken, there was no going back. Although Paul had his call to preach to the Gentiles before Peter did, it was Peter who first made the inclusion of Gentiles a public issue and took it right to the heart of the church leadership in Jerusalem, because he wanted it officially recognized. There were times, of course, when he wavered in this commitment, as when he visited Paul in Antioch. At first he was happy to sit and eat with the Gentile believers, but when some Jewish believers arrived from Jerusalem, he lost his nerve and sat apart (Galatians 2:11–14). However, whereas Paul developed his mission among the Gentiles and taught equality before God (Galatians 3:28; Ephesians 2:14), it was largely Peter's courage in facing his own prejudices and those of his fellow Jews that brought about the climactic change in the growth of the Church, probably saving it from becoming an obscure Jewish sect which might have eventually died out like all those before it.

Making it personal

One vision was given to a Gentile who acted with certainty and determination; the other to a man who, although a leader in the church in Jerusalem, had a track record of making hasty decisions and not following them through. It was Peter who got carried away with enthusiasm on the Mount of Transfiguration when he heard the dialogue between Jesus and Moses and Elijah He wanted to stay on the mountain in an unrealistic bid to keep in touch with wonder (Mark 9:2–8). For his trouble God sent a divine fog which obliterated everything but Jesus. It was Peter who tried to protect Jesus from his own future when Jesus told him that he would be put to death but would later rise. Moments earlier he had received a prophetic insight from God about the true identity of Jesus as the Son of God, but it had gone to his head and he thought he knew everything now. When Jesus prophesied his own death, Peter decided that it was time to rescue him from his depression. For his arrogance he was told he was acting just like Satan! (Matthew 16:13–23). It was Peter who boasted in the upper room that he would never deny Jesus and went to the prayer meeting in Gethsemane with a sword strapped to his side because he meant business (Luke 22:31–38). It all came to a bitter end with the crowing of the cock and the weeping Peter running fearfully out into the night.

We would be more than a little hesitant to think that such a person should be entrusted with so important a calling as to open a new era of ministry in the life of the Church. Our instincts would tell us he was unsafe and that we should expect God to use someone more reliable. Yet Jesus had appointed him the leader of the emerging Church and called him by the new name of 'rock' (Peter) whereas previously his name had been Simon (Matthew 16:18). (No doubt there was a humorous edge to this naming which would not have been lost on the other disciples. Peter, according to his track record, gave the impression of being anything but steady as a rock!) When the women were confronted by angels on the day of resurrection, they were told to go back to Jerusalem and tell the disciples, *including Peter*, the good news (Mark 16:7). The broken man had not been left to spiral down into a pit of darkness and despair. He had been lifted up into new possibilities. By the time the rooftop vision was given to him, Peter had come to a place of greater security in his life and ministry. He had become a well-respected leader and missionary in the Church and his later epistles were to be full of references to being steadfast and having endurance through times of trial and suffering (1 Peter 1:6–7; 2:18–25). You get the definite impression that this writer knew what he was talking about.

We need to be open to the surprising God who can challenge our well-settled ways of living our lives for him, and we need to be ready for new departures of faith. Although it is a rather well-worn statement, one of the points of discussion for the Church in our post-modern society is to find a new way of 'being church'. This is urgent because it is obvious that the young and not-so-young of our day are uninterested in institutionalized religion. They may be interested in Jesus but by and large they are not interested in the Church that carries his name. However, I see a number of fresh initiatives growing in our land as people experiment with the concept of a 'church without walls', what some have called 'cell church' or the 'church that meets in the home'. It is one of the reasons for the revival of interest in Celtic spirituality. People are looking for new spiritual risks and challenges. Not all get it right by any means but they are trying to listen to what the Spirit is saying and go with new movements of God's Spirit. Are there new Peters out there to whom God has given a heart of love and a soul of adventure? Who can stand in the place of vision and see the new things that God wants to do, to bring his care and healing to a broken world?

Prayer

Loving God of the endless age,
renew me by your dream-time touch,
so I'm ready for amazing days
and dance with new and living ways.

Living God of the running waves,
pour your tidal graces through me,
so I'm ready for turbulent days
and dream for new and living ways.
Amen

16

Being in the right place at the right time

Paul's mission directive

We decided to leave for Macedonia at once, for we could
only conclude that God was calling us to preach Good
News there.   *Acts 16:10 (NLT)*

The dream

That night Paul had a vision. He saw a man from Macedonia
in northern Greece, pleading with him, 'Come over here and
help us!'   *Acts 16:9 (NLT)*

By now we should be getting familiar with the experience of vision
and dream interlocking with each other during sleep. Together they
form one of the classic ways in which God brings his guidance
into our lives. It is our loss that we have not learnt to understand
all the ways in which God works and to be open to them for ourselves. I often ask the question, 'Apart from Christmas, when was
the last time you had a sermon in your church on dreams?' Or
perhaps I should ask, 'When was the first time?' Usually the answer
is 'Never.' We need to ask God to help us recover an openness to
his speaking to us in our sleep and revealing his will for us through
visions. One thing is certain: after the apostle Paul had received
his first vision experience on the road to Damascus, he had an
expectancy that God would guide him again and again in this way.

Not long after his conversion, when he had returned to Jerusalem,
Paul was warned in a dream to leave the city immediately because

his life was in danger (Acts 22:17–21). Paul records in his letter to the largely Gentile congregation in Galatia that he later went up to Jerusalem 'by revelation' (Galatians 2:1–2) to explain why he had redirected his mission to the Gentiles. The word here for 'revelation' is *apokalupsis*, and it means to 'unveil' or 'disclose'. It strongly suggests that this was a vision or dream experience in which God spoke to him and showed him what he had to do. On another occasion, he was having a hard time preaching in the city of Corinth and had decided to give up and go somewhere else. He was facing mounting opposition from zealous Jews who thought he was preaching heresy. Paul had a vision in his sleep in which God told him not to be afraid to speak out for the Lord, that he would be protected and, most importantly of all, that there were people waiting to hear and respond to what he had to say (Acts 18:9–11). The result was that Paul stayed on for a further eighteen months and established a church in Corinth. Out of it poured a ministry and a witness that spread over Europe and Asia.

Years later, Paul was once again facing a howling mob in Jerusalem, bent on killing him. This time he was officially arrested, possibly for his own safe-keeping, until he had faced the charges before him. He had tried to explain his mission to the hostile crowd but they were enraged and violence exploded around him. Consequently he was bundled back into gaol and must have thought that everything was turning dark and hopeless. All the promise of mission and travel now seemed to be over and his witness no longer of any value. Yet God came to Paul in a dream vision in the night and prophesied that he would speak for Jesus in Rome. He was not finished yet! (Acts 23:11).

The final dream vision given to Paul was in the middle of a storm at sea that threatened the lives of everyone on board ship. Just as they had all given up hope, the shackled prisoner on board calmed their hearts, although not the storm. Paul told them that the ship was definitely going to sink but that an angel of God had appeared to him in his dream and assured him that everyone would be saved. The ship would be wrecked upon an island and they would all survive. Every word he spoke came true (Acts 27:21–26).

We can see that Paul had learned to recognize the word of the Lord in his dream visions and, as a consequence, the Church was encouraged and established in the teeth of opposition. We should likewise cultivate a sensitivity to God speaking to us when we sleep. I would encourage you to offer your sleep and dreams to God before you go to bed. It is standard practice for us to commit our way to the Lord when we begin the day, so why not do it at the end of the day—God does not stop speaking to us just because we go to sleep!

The story behind the dream

The immediate background to this dream vision of Macedonia seems to be frustration. Somehow things were not going the missionaries' way, and Paul and Silas felt blocked from working in the towns that they wanted to evangelize. At first everything had gone well. They strengthened the churches in Derbe and Lystra as they headed west on the main highway through Galatia. For reasons we (and possibly Paul and Silas) are not told, they did not follow the road into the province of Asia but turned north towards Bithynia. As they came to the town of Mysia, the Spirit of God once again blocked their journey, so they turned west again and came to the coastal town of Troas, which looked out over the Aegean Sea (Acts 16:1–8). Perhaps by this time they were beginning to wonder if God had new plans which they had not considered before—namely taking the good news of Jesus into brand-new areas, such as Greece. Troas was an ideal place to start.

They would have reflected on the lost opportunities to preach and strengthen the churches in Asia, and perhaps wondered what on earth God was playing at. And as they could go no further west, it was possibly dawning on them what all those closed doors were about. These were the things that were on their minds as they slept that night. For Paul, however, there may have been something else troubling him, even though it is never once mentioned in his letters or speeches—the break-up of his relationship with Barnabas.

Paul and Barnabas had argued about the suitability of John Mark to be a member of their team. He had been part of the first mission but had suddenly deserted them when they were in Asia, and returned to Jerusalem (Acts 13:13–14). As they prepared to go out on mission again, Barnabas, ever the encourager of the broken, wanted to include the runaway John Mark, to give him a second chance. But Paul had not forgotten what Mark had done and had decided that he was not suitable for the work. Barnabas and Paul had had a row over this young man and it broke up their teamwork. Barnabas returned to Cyprus, his homeland, and took John Mark with him; he never worked with Paul again (Acts 15:36–41). Paul teamed up with Silas, who had come from Jerusalem to encourage and support the new Gentile Christians of Antioch. Together they headed out for the very territory and churches that Barnabas had formerly helped to establish. Did Paul think of his old friend with regret when God forbade him to go into areas where he had formerly worked with Barnabas? It could have been that God used these times of saying 'no' to mission not only to guide his workers to where he wanted them geographically but also to where he wanted Paul to be in the attitudes of his heart. There seems to be some evidence for this, because when Paul was languishing in prison some years later, he commended John Mark as someone who was a blessing to him (2 Timothy 4:11). Barnabas, who helped to encourage Paul into ministry, had obviously done a good job with John Mark too: the former runaway stuck by Paul even though Paul had not stuck by him.

As he wondered what was in the mind of God, with all these doors closing to their work, perhaps Paul sifted through his argument with Barnabas and asked God to forgive him for his stupidity towards his old friend. By the time he settled down for the night in Troas, I think God was ready to speak the next step of guidance because Paul was at last ready to take it.

Learning the dream message

The dream picture is simple—a man in the recognized dress of a Macedonian, with an urgent cry for help. The Greek word used here is *parakaleo*, which literally means to 'call someone alongside'. Some more familiar translations are 'comforter', 'exhorter' or 'counsellor'. The same word is used in the Gospel of John to describe the work of the Holy Spirit in the life of the Christian. The Holy Spirit is to be, for all time and for every Christian, what Jesus was for his disciples over a few years (John 14:16). The Holy Spirit is to be our teacher (John 14:26), our witness (John 15:26) and the one who convicts the world of its sin and its need of righteousness, and warns of the dangers of judgment (John 16:7–8).

The dream vision is a prophetic appeal to take the life-saving good news about Jesus into the new mission field of Macedonia, made famous by Philip of Macedon, who set up his capital in Philippi and whose fame was increased by his powerful son, Alexander the Great.

Following the dream

What happened next is related by Luke (co-worker with Paul and author of Acts) as an eyewitness account. This is the first time he appears personally in the narrative and so we must conclude that he joined Paul and Silas and their team in Troas either then or shortly beforehand. Luke says, 'We decided to leave for Macedonia at once' (Acts 16:10). There was no hesitation about whether Paul's vision was a result of too much cheese and wine the night before! By now, Paul was familiar with the ways in which God worked in his life. They crossed the Hellespont on what was to become a roller-coaster ride of witness and miracles, persecution and imprisonment, shipwreck and suffering and eventual death. I well remember my old Bible College principal, Stanley Banks, saying that the life of Paul from this moment on resembled the trail left by a bleeding hare as it raced across the snow. Paul's life and mission were characterized by continuous trials and suffering (see 2 Corinthians 4:8–12; 7:5; 11:23–27). Yet he never looked back from his calling and never really stopped until he was imprisoned for his faith. Even then, he wrote letters that have served the Church ever since.

Making it personal

There is nothing so frustrating as when we try to work for God and find that things do not seem to go the way we had hoped. Something like this would have gone through Paul's thoughts when his way was blocked for the third time. He may have asked, 'What are you playing at, God?' He could have moaned that he had been through all kinds of opposition and persecution to do God's will, so God could at least make sure that the missionary journey went smoothly! Elijah behaved like this. When God finally tracked him down in the desert where he had almost died of starvation, he asked Elijah what he was doing there. Out poured the moans. Elijah told God that he had been very zealous for God's work and had single-handedly faced up to a king and nation who were intent on tearing down every altar that had been set up to God. He went on to say that now he was being hounded for his faith as he was the only faithful witness left in the land (1 Kings 19:3–10, 14). The only thing he didn't do was to blame God for everything going wrong.

Of course we know the rest of the story—that God had 7000 others who were still faithful to him and that things were not as bad as Elijah thought. But God does not tell us everything that we would like to know, and we have to trust him. Paul and Silas, although wondering what God was up to, still trusted their Lord and followed the only options open to them. When things do not work out for us, of course we should voice our concerns, but we should also keep true to God and follow in his ways. When Polycarp, the aged Bishop of Smyrna, was facing execution for his faith and was offered his life if he denied Christ, he gave a memorable reply: 'Eighty-six years have I served him, and he has done me no wrong; how can I blaspheme my king and my saviour?'[1] He would not take the easy route out. We may never know why things go wrong, but it does not make us a failure. As painful and frustrating as a situation may be, it is an opportunity to be still rather than be panicked, a time to make sure of our relationship with God and his hold upon us.

Paul's Macedonian vision is the final dream story in this book, and the lesson it teaches us is that God is looking for people who recognize his voice and rise to do his will. There is a place for wrestling with doubts and uncertainties, but there comes a time for faith to take action. It was Frank Lake, in his seminal book *Clinical Theology*, who said that the thing to be admired about the disciples of Jesus was not so much their powerful experiences but that they were honest doubters. Their doubting was not the place where they abandoned their faith, refusing to move on with God, however. There came a time when, having worked through their problems, they got on with serving the Lord. Gideon too had to move on from testing God with signs. God did not let Elijah brood in his cave but fetched him out with his still, small voice of encouragement (1 Kings 19:11–13). Peter was, no doubt, sitting in a corner of that upper room with his face buried in his hands when the women burst in to say that the Lord had sent them with a personal word of loving greeting for him, and that Jesus was coming to see him (Mark 16:7).

I think it hurts the heart of God that we do not recognize his voice when he speaks to us, because this is an indication of how little intimacy we have cultivated with him. Paul learned how God spoke in dream visions and this understanding took him to the centre of the Spirit's actions for his day and age. We need to ask God to help us to open all parts of our lives to him so that we can hear his voice and do his will. One specific area that this book has concentrated upon is dreams. We should learn to pray that our dreams become for us another place in which we learn to listen to the voice of God in our lives.

Prayer

Wild Spirit of my nights and days,
wake me up with your word of life
so that I might see you,
so that I might serve you.

Jesus Christ, bright and morning star,
walking the highways of my heart
so that I might see you,
so that I might serve you.

Great God of waiting and wonders,
weave your threads of healing in me
so that I might see you,
so that I might serve you,
so that I might celebrate you,
my Lord and my God.
Amen

Epilogue

There are far more dream and vision stories in the Bible than have been covered by this book. My hope is that you are now sufficiently interested to want to read the scriptures, looking with renewed interest for what they have to tell us about being open to God as we sleep and dream. You may now have lots of questions, such as, 'What if I do not remember my dreams?' 'How can I make sure that my dreams are protected from the evil one?' 'How can I correctly interpret my dreams?' Rather than trying to answer them all here, I have included some suggestions for further reading at the end of this book. My other goal in writing this book is to encourage you to respect your dreams but not to make more of them than they are. They are a piece of our own creation and if we learn to offer them to God as a normal part of our lives they may from time to time become the window through which God invites us to look and see something more of his touch upon us and his world of opportunities.

Notes

2 Getting personal with the prophetic: Joseph's home dreams

1 *Commentary on the Old Testament*, Vol. 1, C. F. Keil and F. Delitzsch, Hendrickson, 1989, p. 335.
2 *Commentary on the Old Testament*, p. 335.

3 Dreams in dark places: Joseph in prison

1 For a fuller explanation of the importance and significance of dreams for this period, read the chapter entitled 'The World of Dreams' in my book *Healing Dreams* (Triangle, 1995).
2 There is some debate over the identity of this unnamed disciple who let Peter into the courtyard where Jesus was being interrogated. Some think that it was John, because the incident is mentioned only in his Gospel and he does have the habit of referring to himself in elliptical ways, such as 'the disciple whom Jesus loved' (John 13:23; 21:20).

4 Dreams that demand a response: Pharaoh's recurring dreams

1 Joyce G. Baldwin, 'The Message of Genesis 12—50', *The Bible Speaks Today*, IVP, 1986, p. 174.
2 Quoted in Baldwin, 'The Message of Genesis 12—50', p. 349.

6 Listeners make the best leaders: Samuel's wake-up call

1 Quoted in J. A. Hadfield, *Dreams and Nightmares*, Penguin, 1974, p. 113.

7 Becoming a wise one: Solomon's dream interview

1 William Dement, *The Promise of Sleep*, Pan Books, 1999, p. 41.

9 Seeing the end of all things: Nebuchadnezzar's dream of a multi-metalled man

1 Herman Riffel, *Your Dreams: God's Neglected Gift*, Kingsway, 1984, p. 22.

10 Seeing the Lord of all things: Nebuchadnezzar's testimony to healing and wholeness

1 Donald J. Wiseman, *The Oxford Companion to the Bible*, eds Bruce Metzger and Michael D. Coogan, OUP, 1993, p. 553.

11 A model father: Joseph's marriage dream

1 Riffel, *Your Dreams*, p. 22.
2 *Dioderus Siculus*, 4–9, 1–10.
3 Donald Coggan, *The Servant Son*, Triangle, 1995, pp. 4–5.

12 Saving Jesus: the Christmas warning dreams

1 Gillian Wagner, *Barnardo*, Eyre and Spottiswoode, 1980, pp. 10, 79.
2 Morton T. Kelsey, *God, Dreams and Revelation*, Augsburg Fortress, 1991, p. 7.
3 'Confession 19', in R. P. C. Hanson, *The Life and Writings of the Historical Saint Patrick*, Seabury Press, 1983, pp. 86–87.
4 James Ryle, *A Dream Come True*, Eagle, 1995, pp. 166–170.

13 Nightmare Jesus: the trouble with Pilate's wife

1 Ann Wroe, *Pilate: the biography of an invented man*, Vintage, 2000.
2 Wroe, *Pilate: the biography of an invented man*, p. 36.
3 Wroe, *Pilate: the biography of an invented man*, p. 244.
4 Tony Blair, interview in the *Sunday Telegraph*, 7 April 1996.

14 The man for the moment: Ananias' gift to world mission

1 Joseph Henry Thayer, *Greek–English Lexicon of the New Testament*, Associated Publishers and Authors Inc., 1895, p. 199.
2 Morton T. Kelsey, *God, Dreams and Revelation*, Augsburg, 1974, p. 19.

15 Windows on the world: Peter's rooftop dream

1 W. E. Vine, *Expository Dictionary of New Testament Words*, Vol. 4, Zondervan, 1982, p. 148.

16 Being in the right place at the right time: Paul's mission directive

1 *Ante-Nicene Fathers*, Vol. 1, Hendrickson, 1994, p. 41.

Resources and further reading

Resources

Praying with Dreams, a recording of a live dream counselling session with Russ Parker, is available on CD from the Acorn address below and from the website bookshop, <www.acornchristian.org>.

Dream Seminars: information about day and weekend conferences on dreams led by Russ Parker can be obtained from Acorn Christian Healing Foundation, Whitehill Chase, High Street, Bordon, Hants GU35 0AP. Tel.: 01420 478121.

Further reading

John Beaumont, *God in My Dreams*, Destiny Image, 1987
Graham Fitzpatrick, *Dreams and Visions*, Sovereign World, 1991
Russ Parker, 'Dreams as a Religious Phenomenon', a Master's Degree thesis, 1982. Obtainable on loan from the library of St John's College, Bramcote, Nottingham NG9 3DS.
Russ Parker, *Healing Dreams*, Triangle Books, 1993
Herman H. Riffel, *Voice of God*, Tyndale House, 1978
James Ryle, *A Dream Come True*, Eagle, 1995
John A. Sandford, *Dreams and Healing*, Paulist Press, 1978